# DRAMATIC

EFFECTS with

# ARCHITECTURAL
# PLANTS

# DRAMATIC EFFECTS with

# ARCHITECTURAL PLANTS

Noël Kingsbury

The Overlook Press

Woodstock • New York

First published in the United States in 1997 by
The Overlook Press
Lewis Hollow Road
Woodstock, New York 12498

Library of Congress Cataloging-in-Publication Data

Kingsbury, Noel
Dramatic effects with architectural plants / Noel Kingsbury
1. Landscape plants. 2. Landscape plants—pictorial works.
3. Landscape painting. I. Title.
SB435.K58 1997
712—dc21 96-49535 CIP

ISBN: 0-87951-773-5

*Printed in Spain*

First American Edition
1 3 5 7 9 8 6 4 2

# CONTENTS

# INTRODUCTION

Architectural plants are the skeleton of the garden, the framework, the structure. They can be traditional clipped evergreen hedging plants such as yew, holly or box, or they can be exotic-looking palms and yuccas, majestic perennials commanding the border, or delicate ferns nestling in a shady corner of a bog garden. They are always plants with a distinct and strong form, usually with foliage of beauty and interest as well. Evergreens, present all the time, come winter or summer, are among the more valuable of architectural plants, making a framework and structure for the garden in time as well as in space. The elements of form and structure are just as important in a garden as colour, indeed, many would argue that they are more so. Even gardens that have an essentially informal and naturalistic style such as cottage or wild gardens benefit from something to give them a framework. The architectural plant is there to provide this.

**Architectural plants provide year-round structure and substance; flowers are only part of the story**

For many of us, gardens are primarily about flowers and colour. But flowers are ephemeral, they are here one day and gone the next, and during the days of winter, what is there to look at beyond the occasional snowdrop venturing out into the wind and rain? Even at the height of summer, when the garden is burgeoning with colour and scent, there is a need for structure and form. Without at least a few strong or elegant shapes, something to give height and provide a framework, the garden is liable to sink into a blurred and boneless jelly, too soft-focus and vague. A garden given over entirely to colour can also be restless, offering too much visual stimulation. Areas of green relax the eye, refreshing the senses before the next burst of colour. Foliage can be used as a counterpoint to flowers, but it should also be appreciated in its own right.

▶ Never underestimate the vegetables. Ordinary onions gone to seed can be stylish garden plants. They benefit from a starkly simple setting.

Colour is such a major part of gardening that it can be quite an effort to conceive of planting in other terms. A useful exercise is to look at black and white photographs of gardens; perhaps you should photograph your own in this way, or gardens open to the public that you particularly like. In monochrome, it is the architectural plants that stand out, anything with distinctive foliage or shape. If you compare a colour photograph of the same scene it may surprise you how differently you look at the pictures. In black and white you are drawn

**Do not let the immediacy of dazzling floral colour blind you to the more subtle virtues of fine and sculptural foliage**

to the structural elements that may not be so visible when you are distracted by colour, and it can also show dramatically how nondescript many favourite plants are when they are shorn of their most obvious characteristics. Many fine plantings will be reduced to an indistinct blur, the result of there being too few strongly defined, or architectural, plants that hold the garden together, and too many plants with small, matt leaves. Having undertaken this exercise, you will probably agree that even the most beautiful border with a clear colour scheme will benefit from such analysis, leading perhaps to the decision to make sacrifices amongst the flowers and introduce more structure and form.

Even the best planned flower border will cease to bloom at some point, usually by late autumn. What follows? Without architectural plants a border or planting will be practically lifeless through the winter, and very sparse for much of the spring. Evergreens are vital for keeping a sense of life in the garden through the colder months, and those with strong shapes bring an additional quality to the scene. These last can be shaped by nature, such as the definite upright growth of a cypress or holly, or the mound of elegant leaves formed by hellebores. They can also be created by art, as with clipped topiary yew and box. But architectural shapes do not have to be evergreen. Without their leaves, plants with distinctive shapes, such as large thistly perennials, or plants with elegant patterns of twigs, such as *Nothofagus* (southern beech), can be fully

◀ The contrast between pendant laburnum flowers and spherical allium heads is spectacular but short lived. The clipped box balls will be here all year round.

ALLIUM · BUXUS SEMPERVIRENS · TELLIMA GRANDIFLORA

appreciated. And many perennials carry remarkable seed heads throughout the winter. These can look magical when lit by soft, low-angled winter sunlight, and truly stunning when coated by hoar frost.

However, hot summers also reveal the merits of architectural planting (see page 91). When colour cannot be relied upon, foliage, shape and form must become the garden designer's materials. It is not surprising that the origins of European formal gardens lie in the Mediterranean region, where long hot summers make flowering plants rare. Gardeners from northern climes often find it difficult to understand the

**Flowers and colour in nature are a luxury, greenery and foliage a necessity. Perhaps this should make us re-examine their roles in the garden**

sheer practicality of that supremely architectural of garden styles, the Renaissance Italian; I remember my father on the hedged slopes of the Boboli gardens in Florence exclaiming 'this is not a garden'. The fact is that only drought-tolerant shrubs and trees will survive a Mediterranean summer and most of these are evergreen with no dormant period.

▲ Hoar frost is like a magic wand that transforms even relatively dull plants into things of beauty. It has the effect of enhancing and outlining both overall shape and detail.

Formality versus informality is one of the greatest and oldest debates in gardening. The formal tradition has had an immense effect on garden history, with creators of gardens either developing and furthering it, or reacting against it so strongly that they aim to create gardens that are totally naturalistic in inspiration and appearance. Many now favour a compromise; they may grow plants informally in natural arrangements, but they retain some elements of the formal tradition to give architectural structure: clipped hedges, tightly trained columns, some topiary and so on. There is little doubt that the creative tension caused by the interweaving of the two traditions is not only very pleasing but widely appreciated.

▶ *Cotoneaster horizontalis* is a well known garden shrub, with a unique pattern of branching. By giving each one a white outline, frost has made a feature of the leaves too.

**COTONEASTER HORIZONTALIS · ECHINOPS · NOTHOFAGUS**

◄ Plants should be looked at close to as well as from afar. The rewards, particularly the details of leaves, can be great. This is a portion of a *Gunnera manicata* leaf.

While Classical gardens rely for their effect on regular clipping into the desired geometrical shapes, more modern gardens in regions that experience hot, dry summers often use quite a different approach. Garden designers in California, for instance, have spearheaded the use of the dramatic foliage of desert and semi-desert plants, such as yuccas and agaves. Their flowering season may be fleeting, but the bold foliage more than compensates for this. Succulents, plants native to these conditions, are supremely sculptural and offer endless creative opportunities for the artistic gardener.

**Garden designers argue incessantly about formal versus informal gardens. In fact, architectural plants are just as important in both**

This brings us to what is perhaps one of the most important reasons why architectural plants should be promoted, and that is water conservation. The North European garden tradition of roses, bedding plants, flowering shrubs and verdant lawns is one that relies on a reasonably humid climate. Transplanted across the world it can only be maintained by copious amounts of watering. It is not surprising that water reserves have fallen to critically

ACANTHUS SPINOSUS · AGAVE · DARMERA PELTATA · ERYNGIUM GIGANTEUM

low levels in many regions. Gardeners in many areas are having to explore new ways of creating beautiful gardens without putting pressure on precious water resources.

**Gardeners in dry climates should not complain, but be grateful! They can grow the widest range and most dramatic of architectural plants**

Using plants that thrive naturally in drier climates is one answer. Another is to build gardens around plants whose interest lies in their form and foliage, rather than flowers. Dry climates fortunately produce many more architectural plants than humid ones, giving the adventurous gardener endless scope for experimentation.

Even in cooler, humid climates there are gardeners who have problems with dry soils, for example, those who work on light sands or hot, dry banks. In such situations the hardiest species native to a Mediterranean climate may be selected to create exciting, low maintenance planting schemes built around architectural plants, contrasted with low hummocky shrubs like cistus, sage and lavender. In this way, a problem has been turned into a blessing with the creation of a garden that evokes exotic, faraway places.

There is no doubt that architectural plants have become more fashionable over the years, as a greater awareness of form and foliage has grown among gardeners. This has been stimulated in part by an interest in garden traditions that rely less on floral colour. The greatest influence has come from traditional Japanese gardens, especially designs which encompass small, unpretentious courtyards. These have inspired many garden designers to create wonderfully simple compositions for shady areas around buildings, using foliage plants such as ferns, bamboos and hostas. The relatively limited palette found in both Japanese and classical European formal gardens makes us concentrate on the forms of the plants, the texture of leaves, the patterns of light and shadow cast

▲ **Try to forget about flowers occasionally. Learn to look at plants in different ways and from new angles, appreciating the detail of leaves and the subtleties of seed heads.**

EUPATORIUM PURPUREUM · GUNNERA MANICATA · YUCCA GLORIOSA

◄ You are being told very clearly here 'look straight ahead'. Such strong direction creates a clear structure for a garden, but notice also how the hedge creates a sense of expectation by hiding the next part of the garden from sight.

by twigs and stems, and the interaction between contrasting shapes. These gardens also make us more aware of the myriad shades of green to be found in the plant world.

In this book I aim to look at how architectural plants can be used in different kinds of garden, from the very formal to the purely naturalistic. They can be used simply as elements in a design to provide the bones for a predominantly floral planting, or they can be made much more central to the whole project, a garden whose whole atmosphere relies upon carefully chosen foliage, a range of forms and a variety of contrasting or complementary textures.

These plants are called 'architectural' because they add constructional elements to the garden. Often a direct analogy is made between the garden and buildings, for example, the way that the sub-divisions of classic English gardens (such as Vita Sackville-West's Sissinghurst in south-east England) are referred to as 'rooms'. The hedges, of course, are the walls and the gaps in them the doors and windows. High hedges direct the eye very definitely and thus control the vista one sees. But plants can also be used more subtly to entice the viewer to look in a particular direction. Avenues of trees or shrubs and striking 'eyecatcher' plants are excellent examples of this kind of control. These aspects of planting are dealt with in the chapter 'Vista and Framework'.

**Classical and Japanese gardens may seem very alien, but they are an important source of inspiration to the gardener interested in using form**

'Shape and Form' covers the variety of ways in which structural plants are used in gardens, from the very formal and traditional uses of geometrically clipped bushes, the training of standards and the attention to elaborate topiary, to the naturalistic garden where entirely natural shapes are used to give structure to borders and wildflower meadows.

'Foliage and Texture' aims to encourage gardeners to look at leaves, branches and twigs, the elements that will give pleasure for many more days than floral displays. 'Location and Ambience' explores how architectural plants

**ARUNDARIA · CHUSQUEA CULEOU · HOSTA · PHYLLOSTACHYS**

can be selected to create a particular look. For example, there are a number of completely hardy plants that look tropical or exotic. Using them can transform your garden from a suburban backyard into a rainforest!

The 'Plant Directory' aims to cover the most important and useful architectural plants, from traditional to new and novel species, from classically formal to uncompromisingly wild. Nearly all are fully hardy, but some rather more tender plants have been included because they are exceptionally beautiful. These will tolerate only light frosts so they may need winter protection in colder climates, or they could be grown in containers that can be moved indoors during the coldest months. They will amply reward this extra care. Finally, an appendix deals with those aspects of cultivation that are particularly relevant to growing architectural plants.

To help give you ideas, each page of this book has some plants listed in capitals at the bottom. These are plants that are pertinent to the discussion in the text, the majority of which will be found in the Plant Directory at the back of the book. This section is designed to introduce the reader to the most important plants with architectural value. In many cases, the plants mentioned will also have close relatives which are just as good, but are perhaps less readily available. This section focuses primarily, but not entirely, on reliably hardy plants. The warmer your climate, the more dramatic the range of foliage plants that you can grow. But, even if you only have a small area of sheltered micro-climate, it is worth being adventurous and trying tender species. Small specialist nurseries often yield better results than large garden centres.

**Next time you go to the garden centre, promise yourself that you won't look at the flowers. You will find yourself looking at plants in a whole new light**

I hope the book will inspire you to look at your garden in a new light. Even if you still consider yourself a 'flower gardener' by the end, you will hopefully realize the benefits of using more foliage, at least, and feel a sense of liberation at the prospect opened up by architectural plants.

▶ Giant hogweed (*Heracleum mantegazzianum*) is one of the largest and most magnificent herbaceous plants. It always gives scale and proportion to its surroundings.

HERACLEUM MANTEGAZZIANUM · STIPA ARUNDINACEA

# 1 VISTA & FRAMEWORK

A garden without a framework is rather like a plate of stew – it may be jolly tasty but you do not spend long looking at it! An array of lovely plants may be great fun to explore, looking at them all individually, smelling them, rubbing aromatic leaves and so on, but, as a whole, the garden will not hold our attention. Just as a carefully prepared and imaginatively garnished dish looks more appetizing and adds to the pleasure of dining, so a few plants with a strong form in carefully considered positions, or some hedges to surround or break up the garden, can make all the difference.

Architectural plants can be used to form boundaries, physical or psychological, which control the way a garden is seen. Strong forms serve to channel vision down particular pathways, drawing attention to certain places and away from others, they even help to determine how quickly the garden is viewed. Framework is an important part of the formal garden tradition, but it is just as important in less formal ones too.

► **Clipped cypresses march into the middle distance, focusing the eye firmly on an 'eyecatcher' palm tree at the end of the vista.**

# VISTAS IN THE GARDEN
## ENCOURAGING EXPLORATION, SHOWING THE EYE WHERE TO LOOK

A vista can be a view from the garden of the neighbouring landscape, or of the garden itself. Every gardener has particular parts of the garden that they want to draw attention to – and maybe some parts or areas beyond that they want to hide.

▲ Clipped evergreens give backbone to the garden in winter, and contrast well with ethereally frosted perennials.

The most obvious way of directing the gaze away is simply to block off the unwanted vista. Hedges, trellis and bulky shrubs are very useful for this, especially evergreens. It may not just be the compost heap you are trying to hide; you may want to screen off part of the garden so that it only becomes visible later on, when you have turned a corner. Part of the skill in garden design is to reveal the garden in stages, making even the smallest garden a journey of discovery, rather than a spectacle that is presented in one go.

Views of the garden, or of the surrounding environment should be revealed in tantalizing snippets before their full glory is seen. For example, gaps between large shrubs, or a hedge with windows cut in it, can reveal a tantalizing and tempting glimpse of the garden beyond, making you want to explore further.

Architectural plants have a key role to play in how the viewer perceives the garden from specific viewpoints. Classic formal gardens achieve this through the use of axes of symmetry.

Avenues are an effective way of creating an axis in a garden, even a small one. An avenue does not have to consist of trees; any plant with a clear shape,

**BERGENIA · FAGUS SYLVATICA · JUNIPERUS SCOPULORUM 'SKYROCKET'**

▲ A hole cut in a hedge (camellia in this case) concentrates the vision wonderfully, giving an enticing view of delights beyond.

preferably evergreen, repeated symmetrically at regular intervals will do the job. The classics are box clipped into pyramids, standard bay 'trees' or columns of yew. Slightly less formal would be narrow conifers such as *Juniperus scopulorum* 'Skyrocket'. Less formal still would be any neat, upright growing shrub such as holly, dramatically shaped plants like yuccas, or, in a small garden, evergreen perennials, such as bergenias.

One disadvantage with avenues is that they direct the eye rapidly in one direction rather than inviting the eye to take in as much as possible. This drawback can be overcome by arranging plants with distinct form in a more flexible way, creating 'guideline' or zig-zag symmetry, so that the viewer's eye is encouraged to rove from side to side.

LAURUS NOBILIS · TAXUS BACCATA · TILIA · TRACHYCARPUS FORTUNEI

# THE GARDEN FRAMEWORK

## FIRST CREATE THE BOUNDARIES AND COMPARTMENTS, THEN BUILD AROUND THEM

When we buy a picture or a carpet, or any other thing of beauty for the house, we generally think about where it is to go. Only the collector will consider a piece of art in isolation. The same is true of gardens. While there are plant collectors, their gardens are often a mess, and most unattractive to those who do not share their passion. The rest of us place plants according to context, with reference to their background, their neighbours, their closeness to the house or patio or other viewing point. When we stand in the garden centre inspecting a rose bush, for example, we think not only about how it will fit into the garden as it is, or the plan we have in mind for it, but also the effect it will have on the rest of the garden around it, as it comes in and out of flower.

**A hedge is a key ingredient for structural planting; it both contains and focuses the view, creating both physical and psychological boundaries**

As the visual appeal of architectural plants will last longer than plants grown purely or largely for their flowers, they will have a greater effect on their surroundings. Consequently, we can use them to control the visual impact of the garden; they will help us see the garden in a particular way. Manipulation is the name of the game – a skilled designer can effectively control the way we see a garden.

First and foremost comes the garden framework. As a garden designer, are you going to allow us to see out of the garden at all? And what parts do you want us to see from the main viewpoint? Hedges are a highly effective way of screening, either keeping the outside world out with a very high hedge, or drawing the eye inwards, away from the neighbours' spaces, as with a lower boundary hedge.

► Winter light silhouettes the pattern formed by the trunks and branches of the trees making up a beech hedge, contrasting with the simple formality of the outline.

**BUXUS SEMPERVIRENS · CHAMAECYPARIS · LAVANDULA**

Hedges can be informal and loose, or formal and architectural, almost literally so in their likeness to walls. Informal plantings do not have to have informal hedges – as we shall notice several times in this book, informality often looks better within a formal framework. Many of the greatest gardens make effective use of high and geometrically clipped evergreen hedges, usually yew (*Taxus baccata*) in cool climates, Italian cypress (*Cupressus sempervirens*) in warmer. However, evergreens can be dull if you do not want something that looks the same all year

**Even very low hedges can be potent psychological barriers; the horticultural equivalent of a strong outline, a way of saying 'do not step over here'**

round. An alternative that allows for seasonal change, and avoids what might seem oppressively dark in winter, is the use of deciduous trees, such as beech (*Fagus sylvatica*) and hornbeam (*Carpinus betulus*).

High hedges can be used not only to separate the garden from the outside world but to create 'rooms' within the garden itself, each with its own distinct character. This technique reached its high point in twentieth-century English gardens such as Sissinghurst in Kent, south-east England and Hidcote in Gloucestershire, south-west England. As an alternative, low hedges will separate one space from the next but will allow the eye to roam more freely. Box (*Buxus sempervirens*) has been a great favourite for centuries for just such a purpose, its dense growth being perfect for maintaining a trimmed, neat shape. Lavender (*Lavandula* spp.) is popular for an even lower hedge.

An alternative to hedges is wooden trellis, covered with climbers. This can have the height of a tall hedge, but not (unless you grow something very dense and rampant) the impermeability. The growth of climbers tends to be wild and uncontrolled, but on a trellis, especially one attractively and thoughtfully designed, they can be kept tidy.

Another option is the 'fedge', a Victorian invention, rarely seen these days. Here, ivy is encouraged to climb up a wire-netting fence, creating a dense and evergreen hedge. Like any other hedge it needs clipping once a year.

◄ Even as boundaries, hedges can be decorative. Here is a good example of a low box hedge (*Buxus*) used to create a centrepoint.

**CARPINUS BETULUS · FAGUS SYLVATICA · LAVANDULA**

# EXCLAMATION
## MARKS
### INCLUDE THE UNEXPECTED AND YOU WILL ENSURE CONSTANT INTEREST

Most of us would agree, I think, that a flat garden is a dull one – a whole dimension has been missed out. The creation of height is an essential part of garden design and architectural plants are often the best way of achieving this. While there is no shortage of readily available plants that create height, the majority take up a lot of space widthways as well. I am thinking in particular of the bulky shrubs that seem to be the stock-in-trade of many garden centres. Far too large for many gardens, they expand shapelessly in all directions, taking up space that could be used for developing more interesting plantings.

**Strongly vertical plants connect earth and sky, garden and space. More than anything else, they can transform a garden with a sense of thrill and energy**

Narrowly and neatly vertical plants, green and growing exclamation marks, have so many advantages: they provide an extra dimension while allowing planting to be carried right up to their base; they create an impact out of all proportion to the amount of ground they take up and do little to obstruct views; their skilful use creates a sense of soaring elegance, that connection between heaven and earth that is achieved by a church spire or the minaret of a mosque. And they can be used effectively in the smallest garden.

Trees or shrubs that are natural verticals are few and far between, and are often too large for many gardens (such as the well known Lombardy poplar, *Populus nigra* 'Italica'). Upright growers can be made more narrowly vertical, though, by clipping and tying them around with wire. The Irish yew, *Taxus baccata* 'Fastigiata' is often used very successfully like this, and can be kept relatively small.

► The Italian cypress (*Cupressus sempervirens*) is unrivalled for its vertical lines. It is hardier than often thought, so could perhaps be planted more often.

**CUPRESSUS SEMPERVIRENS · TAXUS BACCATA 'FASTIGIATA'**

A whole series of springing exclamation marks can be achieved with a crowning strappy-leaved cordyline. In this case, the sense of verticality is enhanced by a tall, stone container.

The finest verticals that are familiar to us are the Italian cypresses that so often surround old buildings in the Mediterranean. These magnificent trees are a lot hardier than people think, and they should be planted a great deal more in areas where winters are cold but not regularly severe. The commonly grown cypresses of cooler climates are nothing like as narrow and elegant and serve only to remind us of suburbia. An exception might be

CALOCEDRUS DECURRENS · CHAMAECYPARIS LAWSONIANA 'KILMACURRAGH'

*Chamaecyparis lawsoniana* 'Kilmacurragh' and in a large landscape the incense cedar, *Calocedrus decurrens*. Strict verticals for smaller gardens, and very cold ones too, can be found among the junipers. While woody plants such as these are with us all year round, there are also herbaceous plants whose strongly

**A tall, elegant columnar tree will give the garden an airiness that earth bound planting cannot attain. Spire-like flower spikes have a similar temporary effect**

vertical flower spikes add that 'soar to the skies' touch to the garden. Foxgloves are quick and easy to grow, and bring a useful vertical feel to shady places. The creamy cimicifugas, less easy to establish (they like it cool and moist, but well drained), are lovely for early autumn. Red hot pokers (*Kniphofia* spp.), though shorter and slightly dumpier, can do the same in sunny spots. But perhaps the finest of all are eremurus, large bulbous plants that thrive in well drained dry places, especially regions with marked and severely hot, dry climates.

► Yew columns stand on parade. Along with the box hedging at their feet, they frame the more relaxed herbaceous gardening. Such columns are best kept tight with unobtrusive wire.

# EYECATCHER
## PLANTS ARE PLANTS THAT SEIZE THE ATTENTION, TURNING A GLANCE INTO A GAZE

▲ Such skill with the shears instantly seizes the attention. Spirals are one of the most challenging topiary shapes to clip. The design dates back to Roman times.

These are plants that will always make you take a good, long look. Visually exciting species, those with dramatic shapes, or spiky, or exceptionally large leaves are always guaranteed to do this, so are 'out of context' plants, such as the palm tree in a cold climate. Eyecatchers direct the attention, away from the compost heap or the scrapyard next door, or towards a glorious vista.

Eyecatchers make good focal points, providing a neat 'full stop' at the end of a tunnel, allee or avenue. However, they have the disadvantage of perhaps drawing too much attention to themselves too quickly, foreshortening perspective and reducing the appreciation of the rest of the garden. A dramatic plant surrounded by rather quiet beauties is liable to completely overshadow them, but then too many of these eyecatchers will create an impression that is fussy and over-stimulating. Go for balance – an eyecatcher must be complemented by worthy points of interest along the way.

As already noted, hardy palm trees make first class eyecatchers; not only are they an unusual sight in many cooler areas, but they are naturally rather attention seeking. A well placed trachycarpus or chamerops is a wonderful focal point. So too are other reasonably hardy spikies, cordylines, *Phormium tenax*, and, in cold winter climates, yuccas. A somewhat less aggressive look can be had with large-leaved plants like the common fig (*Ficus carica*), or, in damp places, *Gunnera manicata*, or the smaller but totally hardy butterburs (*Petasites* spp.).

► Too often seen in suburban settings too small for it, pampas grass (*Cortaderia selloana*) needs a large landscape to look its, potentially magnificent, best.

**Even the most colourful gardens can benefit from the introduction of dramatic forms – something that is surprisingly different from its neighbours**

**CORTADERIA SELLOANA · FICUS CARICA · PHORMIUM TENAX**

Large-leaved plants tend to be deciduous or herbaceous, which is a bit of a disadvantage, along with the fact that they can look a bit unruly in some settings. Nothing beats the spiky-leaved rosette-growers for the combination of drama and symmetry that makes an ideal focal point plant. The gardener who values formality and symmetry above all will want to use nothing else to create an impact. In cold winter climates only the yuccas and possibly the Chusan palm (*Trachycarpus fortunei*) can be grown permanently outside. As focal points are vital to a successful garden design, it may be worthwhile to use half hardy plants in containers, bringing them under cover for the winter. For this purpose, none are better than agaves, whose perfect symmetry seems made for the classical urns in which they are so often seen, and which instantly creates an atmosphere of Mediterranean and classical sophistication.

**The attention-seeking star plant comes into its own when an eyecatcher is needed – but make sure it is not let down by the chorus of plants around it**

▼ Fennel (this is the bronze variety, *Foeniculum vulgare* 'Purpureum') is invaluable for its soft, matt texture, moderating surrounding colours and shapes that might otherwise clash.

Sheer bulk can be a good eyecatcher, especially if garden informality is the order of the day. Pampas grass (*Cortaderia selloana*) is very effective, evergreen, and in a large landscape can look magnificent, although it can be overwhelming in a small garden. Herbaceous alternatives with a bit more class and elegance include the miscanthus grasses, big perennials like Joe Pye weed (*Eupatorium purpureum*), species of elecampage (*Inula* spp.), macleaya species and, perhaps the best of all, the giant silvery thistle relatives, *Cynara cardunculus* and *Onopordum acanthium*. Being herbaceous, they will survive cold winters too.

To some extent any plant with unusual or elegant foliage makes a good eyecatcher; so does anything with strong form. The vertical plants discussed on pages 28–31

► *Eryngium* is one of the most architecturally useful groups of herbaceous perennials. Their flowers continue to look spikily elegant, long after they have stopped blooming.

**CYNARA CARDUNCULUS · INULA · TRACHYCARPUS FORTUNEI**

focus the attention as much as any. Standards (see page 63), and small, relatively upright growers are perfect for less extensive gardens. Dwarf conifers, though overused to the point of becoming a suburban cliché, make good evergreen eyecatchers, and avoiding any with variegated foliage will make your choice look a bit more sophisticated. Some of the best are the very vertical junipers such as *Juniperus communis* 'Hibernica', or the somewhat taller *J. scopulorum* 'Skyrocket'. They look a bit like miniature versions of the Roman cypress, although they are more suitable for areas with hot, dry climates.

**Be bold with the elegance and drama of outstanding plants. One such well placed plant can make more impact than hours of painstaking garden design**

Topiary is a sure way of making people look. It does not have to be elaborate; a simple column or distinct geometrical shape is all that is needed, something that stands out from the more naturalistic growth patterns of the rest of the garden (see page 57).

Seizing the attention of the viewer is one thing, but it does beg the question of what you are going to do with their attention once you have it. A focal point presumes that its surroundings will be appreciated, which is why the classic agave in an urn works so well, surrounded by strong but simple planting and often ornamental stonework. An eyecatcher must be surrounded by attractive and complementary planting, or point the way onward and outward to a good view, perhaps to another part of the garden that might escape initial attention.

Eyecatchers can be deceptively simple: a stark, clipped shape in a wild garden, for instance, is effective because it is distinctly different to its surroundings. A formal shape in a very informal context is both visually and psychologically challenging.

▼ Spiky plants always stand out, whether in formal settings or, as here, in an informal jungly atmosphere. This is a variegated form of *Cordyline australis*.

► It has become almost a cliché, but there is no denying that an agave in a classical urn is one of the best eyecatcher garden features there is.

AGAVE AMERICANA 'VARIEGATA' · CORDYLINE AUSTRALIS · MUSA BASJOO

▲ Ornamental alliums boast good colours and interesting form, combining well with practically all other plants. Striking to the eye in any garden, they thrive on hot, stony soils.

▼ Unfolding leaves of *Gunnera manicata* are mysterious indeed, a surreal touch to the springtime bog garden and a clear indication of the magnificence to come.

▲ The smooth cinnamon bark of *Myrtus apiculata* always seems to invite feeling and stroking, so it is something that needs planting where the trunk is accessible.

◄ The rheums, ornamental rhubarbs, are very easy and rewarding plants, although their size can make them a little out of place in the smallest gardens.

▼ Gardening in mild, maritime areas allows for experimentation with a wide variety of plants that have large and interesting foliage, such as this cordyline.

# BUILDINGS AND PLANTS
## WORK WITH THE SOLID STRUCTURES YOU HAVE, COMPLEMENTING AND COMBINING AS YOU GO

▲ Hard surfaces such as walls and paving are quite demanding visually. They can be either softened by hazy romantic planting, or counterbalanced with other strong forms.

There can be few sights that express grandeur more eloquently than a Baroque, Palladian, or Georgian building surrounded by classically formal gardens. In acknowledging period garden styles, you do not have to be a slave to historical exactitude. A few little references, however, like the occasional clipped shrub, do help to tie a period house and garden together.

Houses, of whatever period, never stand alone from the gardens that surround them. But even if you do not feel that the house demands a particular garden style, there is the problem of the immediate surroundings of the building, the walls that meet the garden, or those areas of paving which you feel need something green.

**Where house meets garden is an excellent opportunity for sympathetic planting, ensuring a smooth transition between brick, branch and leaf**

In fact, houses do create problems for plants, either casting shade or reflecting heat, while their foundations deny a good root run.

To hide the bottom of the walls look at the section on evergreens (page 82) for some new ideas. Alternatively, familiar species such as yews and box may be given a new, more artistic life by imaginative clipping. Even topiary is a possibility. While planting against walls helps to blur the distinction between building and garden, climbers can do more to actively involve architecture in the garden. Climbers that hug walls tightly, such as virginia creepers (*Parthenocissus* spp.) and ivies (*Hedera* spp.) are the neatest.

CEANOTHUS · MAGNOLIA GRANDIFLORA · PARTHENOCISSUS

Planting around buildings does require choosing species that will thrive in the special conditions that walls create. A wall that faces the sun seems an inhospitably hot and dry environment, yet this might be the ideal site for a slightly tender shrub, one that will benefit from the protection of the wall and relish the reflected heat. Warm-wall shrubs can take up a lot of space, but it is possible to clip them into architectural shapes that serve as green buttresses, effectively linking house and garden. The various species and varieties of ceanothus are among the best, flowering deep blue in early summer, especially those with glossy dark green foliage such as *C. impressus* or *C. thrysifolius*. Sheltered walls are ideal for other, more exotic looking shrubs, such as acacias, or large-leaved magnolias, such as *M. grandiflora*. One wall shrub that can be kept clipped very tight, and is tolerant enough to grow on draughty as well as warm walls, is pyracantha. It can be trained and pruned into pillars, columns and archways to complement the building against which it grows.

The opposite problem to the hot dry wall is the sunless cold one. Shade loving plants such as ferns and hostas may well be the answer, particularly evergreen ones. A dry, rubble-filled soil may be a further problem, requiring the selection of plants that will tolerate drier shade, such as the sedge, *Carex pendula*, *Euphorbia amygdaloides robbiae* and the polystichum ferns.

► A tudor house almost begs for a cottage garden full of pastel colours, but using an occasional vertical form helps to give structure and perspective to the garden.

# 2 SHAPE & FORM

Some plants have such strong form that they could almost have leapt off a drawing board; others are so unruly in their patterns of growth that they seem to be doing it deliberately to annoy tidy-minded gardeners. The former can be relied upon to give structure to our gardens with little effort – even placing them at random adds a bit of 'backbone'. But with a bit of effort even the messy growers can be knocked into shape; judicious pruning, clipping and training can turn them into structural plants, too. Combining plants of different shapes, whether natural or artfully created, is a crucial part of garden making – we must feel that the end result is harmonious and interesting.

The classical, formal and the Japanese traditions rely for much of their impact on combinations of different shapes, and often these shapes are heavily manipulated. But, thanks to the diverse growth patterns of many different plants, there is scope for a more naturalistic interpretation.

► The result of much skilled work with a hedge trimmer! In a formal garden, the slightest inconsistency soon stands out.

# ELEGANCE AND GRACE

UPRIGHT, SINUOUS AND STYLISH:
INCLUDE PLANTS THAT ADD
SOPHISTICATION TO A SCHEME

Elegance: one of those words that is difficult to define, but we all know what it means when we see it! The soaring Italian cypress has it, bamboos usually have it (but not the dumpy ones with coarse leaves), some pines have it: older Scots pines (*Pinus sylvestris*) or the Japanese pine (*P. parviflora*) – the one that looks as if it has come off a willow-pattern plate. *Alchemilla mollis*, the common and sometimes rather invasive garden perennial, may look very graceless at first, but look closely at the leaves, their perfect proportions, pleasingly scalloped shape and the way that water runs off them in silvery beads like mercury. That, I think, is elegance.

Like any aspect of beauty, elegance lies in the eye of the beholder. What may seem the epitome of grace to one person may be ungainly to another. Yet certain plants do seem to be almost universally acclaimed as having this quality. The Japanese have perhaps the most finely attuned sense of the elegant, and they originally selected many of the most graceful plants in our gardens for cultivation: many bamboos, ferns, the ginkgo tree and the slow growing maple, *Acer palmatum*, with its finely cut leaves and branches that develop such an interesting zig-zag shape in older trees.

**Difficult to pin down, elegance is a quality that will stay with a visitor when they have appraised a well-considered garden**

The shape of tree branches is particularly noticeable in winter. Among the most notable are the dogwood, *Cornus controversa*, with its unique pattern of layered 'wedding cake' branches, and *Nothofagus antarctica* and *N. dombeyi*, with their intriguingly neat arrangement of twigs and branches. Evergreens that have sculptural, open patterns of branches with beautiful bark include species of arbutus, eucalyptus and the pines.

► Quintessentially elegant, a Japanese maple develops a distinctive slightly zig-zag branching style as it ages, complementing the finely cut, hand-shaped leaves.

**ACER PALMATUM · CORNUS CONTROVERSA · NOTHOFAGUS**

◄ Pampas grass may be bulky but it has undeniable grace, especially when the sun catches the plume-like flowers.

Sculptural, rather than elegant, might be the best description of those plants that take non-linear branching to the extreme: the corkscrew trees, of which the best known are the contorted hazel, *Corylus avellana* 'Contorta', and contorted willow, *Salix babylonica* 'Tortuosa'. Their extraordinary twisted branches are greatly appreciated by some, but not all, gardeners, although most would agree that their pendant, soft yellow catkins are a graceful sight in late winter and early spring.

Bamboos and certain other of the larger grasses are extremely useful for introducing a note of elegance into the garden – something to do with the way the stems bend over slightly towards the tips, the hang of the leaves and the way they move in the slightest breeze. Bamboos are linked inextricably in the popular imagination with the Orient, so the sight of a group in a garden tends to lead the visitor to look for little curved bridges, lanterns and other eastern clichés. This is a shame; they are such beautiful plants that they deserve to be used in a variety of different contexts.

Elegance on a smaller scale is less to do with the overall shape of the plant than with the form and proportions of the leaves. *Alchemilla mollis* has already been mentioned. Its soft green flowers will never overshadow the charm of its leaves, an attribute typical of the best foliage plants, such as macleayas or *Melianthus major* which have rather dull flowers. If their floral beauty were more beguiling, we might miss out on their leaves. Shady corners, in courtyards or around doors by sunless walls, are among the places where it is possible to play with some of the most lovely leaf combinations, making use of both

**Elegance and grace are always worth pursuing. In the subtlest way, they give order to a setting**

ferns and woodland plants (see page 100). Soft light and an absence of colourful flowers enable us to concentrate on their true beauty. Grasses and sedges are some of the most elegant plants, and much underrated. They are particularly useful for adding softness to a planting, and the arching flower and seed heads of the majority of species add grace and delicacy.

ALCHEMILLA MOLLIS · CORYLUS AVELLANA 'CONTORTA' · MELIANTHUS MAJOR

# THE PSYCHOLOGY OF SHAPE

### HOW THE SHAPE OF PLANTS DIRECTLY AFFECTS THE MOOD OF THE GARDEN

Gardening is about psychology, creating environments that manipulate emotions to make the garden user or visitor feel relaxed or stimulated or to give them a sense of escape. Just as colours have an effect on our moods – red is drama, blue is cooling, pink relaxed and cosy – so do shapes. The use of different shapes in the garden can help to create or enhance a particular state of mind, especially if attention is also paid to how they interract with colour and space. Needless to say, people's tastes vary wildly; there are no rights and wrongs – what you do should feel right for you.

**Use plant shapes to create the mood you want, from spiky and dramatic, to soft, bubbly and soothing, or severe and geometrically abstract**

Plants that have clearly defined shapes create a much greater impact on the eye than ones whose shapes we cannot put a name to, or amorphous plants whose habit of growth seems blurred at the edges. A garden composed entirely of plants with non-specific, loose growth patterns, can sometimes be interpreted as vague and formless. In a wild garden this does not matter, but in most borders it does. The addition of a few distinct shapes does a tremendous amount for the overall character of the planting. For example, the ubiquitous dwarf conifer could be used in original combinations, with wispy ornamental grasses and sedges, or evergreen ground covers like species of acaena and lamium. The colours of dwarf conifers and evergreen New Zealand sedges (such as *Carex testacea* or *C. comans*) are from the same palette and their cultural needs are similar, thus making them natural planting companions.

For many people, the term 'architectural plant' actually means one that has an imposing and dramatic form: yuccas and palms, for example. Spiky

► Somewhat reminiscent of chess pieces, olde worlde topiary shapes like these are effective because they combine an obvious display of skill with simplicity.

CAREX TESTACEA · IRIS · TAXUS BACCATA · YUCCA

foliage, as with yuccas and the sword shaped leaves of irises, comes across to most people as dynamic and restless, perhaps aggressive too (especially if you have ever been impaled upon a yucca!). Foliage that radiates from a central point, as with the pleated fans of palms or rosette plants like phormiums, also gives a feeling of movement. Many of these plants need a climate where winters are not regularly severe; if you live in such a climate, they can be combined with a large number of other distinctively sculptural plants that thrive in these conditions: agaves, aloes, echeverias and the hardier prickly pear cacti, such as *Opuntia phaeacantha*. A combination of such strong shapes can easily seem overstimulating, especially if brightly coloured flowers are involved as well. In climates with strong sunlight, bright colours are not a problem, but where grey skies are more frequent they may seem overpowering in contrast.

**Combining different plant shapes in the garden can be as rewarding as combining different colours, and the results will give pleasure over a longer period**

Reducing the amount of contrast between plants by concentrating on a particular repeated shape is a way of making a garden feel more relaxing. Rounded plants are especially soothing; the globular shapes that can be achieved by regular clipping of shrubs have a gently sculptural, cuddly, indeed, almost comic impact. Some plants grow naturally like this anyway, into almost perfect spheres, at least if they are not crowded by neighbours or affected by a strong, single light source. *Hebe* 'Boughton Dome' is one such example. It will slowly form a friendly-looking, evergreen dome that is sprinkled with small white flowers in summer.

The forms of herbaceous perennials are worth considering too. Whilst few have the distinctly defined shapes of woody plants, not all are sprawling and untidy. In fact, because of the seasonal way that they grow, their shape will change as the year progresses. Sternly upright thistles, verbascums and teasels form an excellent contrast with soft, mound-forming grasses and hardy geraniums, or tidy clumps of hostas.

◄ Spiky yuccas always look good in terracotta pots. Together they create a subtle hint of the Mediterranean.

AGAVE · HEBE 'BOUGHTON DOME' · OPUNTIA PHAEACANTHA · PHORMIUM

# DISCIPLINING THE UNRULY
### BRINGING ORDER TO UNTIDY PLANTS, EXPERIMENTING WITH SHAPE IN THE GARDEN

How often is it that we buy a shrub for one feature alone, usually for its flowers, and then find that once it settles down in the garden it sinks in our estimation because of its poor shape, untidily sprawling over its neighbours or dominating a plant grouping? Forsythia, for example, which we love in late winter for its flowers that brighten grey days, is a gangly mass of shapeless branches and weedy leaves for the other eleven months of the year. In a large garden it can be hidden or surrounded by later blooming plants, but in a small one we are rather stuck.

▼ 'Pleaching' is the art of cutting a hedge so that the trunks are visible. Here there is a second lower hedge so that a solid screen is formed.

One of the answers to such quandaries is to restrain such awkward growers through pruning and training. They are never going to be in the first run of architectural plants, but they can play a more positive role in the garden for a larger part of the year if they are controlled. Practically all shrubs can be clipped into some sort of shape, which may be simply a tidy up, or it could be something more sculptural. It is vital to consult a pruning manual before doing this, as flowering may be prevented if plants are pruned at the wrong time of year (see page 141). Many, forsythias included, can be trained into standards (see page 63) or, less ambitiously, trained against walls or fences (see page 141).

It is one thing to keep a woody plant restrained through judicious pruning, but another to actually sculpt it in the way that box, yew, beech and many others are for formal hedging and topiary. In theory it is possible to do this with any tree or shrub, though in practice the denser the pattern of growth the more satisfactory the results will be. Slower growing species tend to be better as well, and are certainly less work. Gardeners need to be more imaginative in the range of trees and shrubs they clip into shapes, experimenting with plants other than the traditional varieties. For example, a garden designer I know has clipped the popular but frequently raggedy silver-leaved weeping pear, *Pyrus salicifolia* 'Pendula', into pillars – very architectural and effective. Such sculptural possibilities offer effective solutions to the frequent problem of what to do with shrubs that threaten to get too big in small gardens. Flowering may be reduced a bit, but their new shape will give them architectural interest for the whole year.

**Do not be daunted by a worthy but unruly plant: appropriate pruning can tame it, so adding to its appeal, especially in the smaller garden**

The possibilities open to the imaginative gardener are endless; the vast majority of clipped shrubs repeat traditional formal patterns, but the creative should experiment with other ideas. Contemporary abstract sculpture is a good source of inspiration. Modern, fluid shapes could be made to echo the natural patterns of the garden.

**FAGUS SYLVATICA · FORSYTHIA · PYRUS SALICIFOLIA · TILIA**

# TOPIARY AN ART FORM
## IMPOSING OR WITTY, TRIMMED AND TRAINED PLANTS ARE EXCELLENT IN AN ARCHITECTURAL DESIGN

Topiary is one of the oldest of garden practices, dating back to Roman times, if not earlier. It is also one of the more controversial techniques, experiencing dramatic ups and downs in popularity over the centuries. Its high point was in sixteenth- and seventeenth-century Europe, but by the early eighteenth century much was destroyed in the rush to create 'landscape gardens'. In Latin countries – Spain, Italy and France – topiary never lost its popularity. The nineteenth century saw a revival of interest in many places, which has continued to the present day.

Topiary is supremely 'architectural' and although we tend to associate it with very formal gardening styles, this need not be the case. Those who dislike topiary on the grounds that it is 'unnatural' should consider the gardens that use it in close proximity to wildflower meadows, or where it punctuates rather chaotic cottage garden borders. The creative tension brought about by such juxtapositions is, to my mind, one of the most effective that the gardener can develop. Hedges and topiary make a wild garden look intended, rather than simply a failure to mow the lawn, while burgeoning natural growth draws attention to the skill involved in making the occasional topiary shapes. Using a small number of clipped forms in a garden can do a tremendous amount to give a sense of structure to a place.

The traditional materials for topiary are yew and box, and in warmer climates the Roman cypress (*Cupressus sempervirens*). These trees grow relatively slowly and have a dense, twiggy habit that lends itself to intricate pruning. Box is very slow growing, which makes it best suited to low shapes and sculptures; yew is faster and is probably the best all round material for the

**Perhaps the most extreme expression of architectural planting, topiary can bring a touch of Versailles or cottage charm to any garden**

◄ **An elderly clipped yew has an interesting combination of geometry and sculpturally gnarled branching.**

**BUXUS SEMPERVIRENS · CUPRESSUS SEMPERVIRENS · TAXUS BACCATA**

► Clipping birds and animals
from yew is a tradition
centuries old. It adds a patina
of age to the garden of the
older house, but can look twee
in more modern settings.

aspiring topiarist. The cypress is better able to cope with hot, dry summers
and can be used to form very intricate shapes, but it has the disadvantage
that its branches have a strong tendency to sweep upwards. Hollies are good,
especially *Ilex crenata*, the traditional topiary material in Japan. Faster
results can be obtained with plants that grow more quickly but still have a
dense habit, for example, *Lonicera nitida* and the conifer *Thuja plicata*.
These, though, will need clipping more often than the traditional plants.

The great thing about topiary is that it is so versatile; the gardener is not
nearly so dependent on the growth habit of the plant but can create whatever
forms are wanted. Popular topiary (rather than the grand, stately home

**From classical obelisks to candy twists, stylized birds to witty sheep, topiary can set the tone of a garden**

variety) shows the vast range of special effects
that can be created: rabbits, peacocks and so
on. The thought of these, and the work
involved in making them, may well fill many
readers with horror, but they serve to illustrate
the possibilities. The modern gardener may
want to work with abstract shapes, which will also be easier to manage.

Topiary's versatility allows plants to be trimmed into the most
architectural of shapes, the straight lines and geometry of buildings,
unattainable with any other living material. No wonder, then, that it has
always been popular as an accompaniment to architecture, becoming a
green extension of the bricks and mortar. Buildings of any grandeur are
greatly enhanced by clipped hedges and topiary, which need not neccessarily
follow the traditional format of symmetry. The abstract shapes used in such
gardens are relatively easy to form: columns, spheres, pyramids.

More complex are the type of representational sculptures mentioned
above that tend to be found around country cottages. They often require a
great deal of skill and many years to make and, clever though they are, can
end up looking somewhat comical. But perhaps this element of humour  is
one of topiary's greatest assets.

**ILEX CRENATA · LONICERA NITIDA · THUJA PLICATA**

# THE MARCH OF THE STANDARDS

## THESE DELICATE CREATIONS MAKE THE MOST OF A FORMAL IDEAL

◄ A huge variety of trees and shrubs can be trained as standards; messy growers like forsythia are particularly rewarding to train.

Standards are a key element of the classical formal tradition. They do not meet with universal acclaim, as many gardeners feel that they look artificial, especially when used *en masse*. Yet, when used sparingly, they can be effective in a variety of different settings.

A standard is a tree, or more usually a shrub, that normally produces multiple stems but which has been trained to have a single stem. In the classical tradition the head is kept clipped, so that the end result is geometrical. The strongest stem is selected, all others cut away and the side shoots removed, leaving a head at the desired height (see page 141). However, there is another kind of standard which is arguably even more artificial, the 'top-worked graft'. These are bushy shrubs which are grafted on top of the straight stems of another related variety. Standard roses are the best known example, but many others are produced as garden centre novelties.

**Standards need not be twee; a neat, healthy specimen or a cheering group can surprise and delight the eye**

Standards make excellent centrepieces. A small standard bay in a bed of herbs or low perennials surrounded by a box hedge is a popular example. In very formal gardens, standards are often grown in lines to form avenues where the effect is dependent on the trees being identical in size and shape.

In cooler climates, holly and yew are the most frequently grown standards. Bay is very popular as a miniature standard, especially in tubs, and woody climbers such as wisteria and honeysuckle can also be used if they are supported for the first few years, after which the central stem becomes strong enough to be self-supporting. In warmer climates, orange trees are sometimes used, the bright fruit against the dark and glossy leaves being very striking.

**CITRUS · LAURUS NOBILIS · LONICERA NITIDA · WISTERIA**

# BEAUTY IN DEATH
## SILHOUETTES OF FROSTED SEED HEADS HAUNT A STARK WINTER SCENE

▲ Frozen and soon to perish; these anthemis flowers are enhanced by a sharp hoar frost, which will be their swan song.

The worst time in the garden is probably early winter; the flowers of autumn are over, the spring ones are a long way off, the leaves have fallen and the berries on fruiting shrubs are being rapidly eaten by birds. However, those gardeners who leave the dead stems and seed heads of summer's border perennials can admire the subtle beauty of what remains.

Once dead, and bleached shades of brown and yellow, the remains of perennials can be appreciated as pure form, as wispy leaves and grasses stand next to prickly or spherical seed heads. Ornamental grasses are appreciated at this time for the variety of forms that their seed heads take.

While leaves tend to become mushy and fall away, seed heads are harder and more durable. Their shapes have an increasing prominence in the garden as the winter months draw on, from the clustered verticals of plants such as *Veronica longifolia* and *Veronicastrum virginicum*, to the flat-headed, rounded bunches of such as achilleas. But it is the tight globular heads, mostly members of the daisy and scabious families (*Compositae* and *Dipsacaceae*) that are the most valuable.

The spherical heads of globe thistles or close-shaped eryngiums are among the best and the oval-shaped seed heads of teasel (*Dipsacus fullonum*) will survive into the following year. Plants such as the tall opium poppy, which has seed capsules that look decorative, are valuable too.

Cold, crisp climates, where the dead stems of perennials are effectively freeze-dried, offer longer-lasting displays than regions where prolonged rain and wind render everything soggy. But, even if autumn gales do limit the effect, we should still delay the annual cut-back until late winter, as perennial and grass seed heads are a valuable source of food for seed-eating birds.

► Plants of a thistly mien, like this eryngium, are especially dramatic in winter. Most have hard foliage that stands up well to bad weather.

## DIPSACUS FULLONUM · ERYNGIUM · VERONICA LONGIFOLIA

# 3 FOLIAGE & TEXTURE

Flowers can have a fleeting presence in the garden, yet they get nearly all the attention, which is most unfair on the rest of the plant. Most of us are all too easily carried away by the siren song of colourful but short-lived flowers, leading us to ignore the potential of leaves (and stems, trunks and bark). Foliage has a much longer season and its handsome appearance is more dependable than flowers.

In a small garden or a key area of larger grounds this is a great advantage. When planning such areas we should perhaps consider the foliage first and put flowers second. Foliage and, to some degree, flowers too, contribute to 'texture', the overall visual appearence of a plant. A plant can appear glossy or matt, hard or soft, plain with large leaves and boldly-shaped flower clusters, or finely detailed with small leaves and tiny flowers. All these aspects are an important part of the way we perceive the garden at first glance.

► Adaptable enough to grow in most soils, ornamental rhubarbs relish the moist ones. Their grandeur is perhaps best appreciated when they are not surrounded by other plants.

# FOLIAGE THE KEY TOOL

## LEAVES ARE AT THE HEART OF ARCHITECTURAL PLANTING, SO USE THEM WELL

Foliage, like flower, can be appreciated at a number of levels. Close up, the subtleties of veining, shape and surface texture are all important; from further away, the character of individual leaves becomes less noticeable but the overall effect created by hundreds or thousands of them becomes a major consideration in the garden as a whole. Leaves *en masse* have visual texture; reflecting light in different ways. This texture is the background for the rest of the garden.

**Foliage is a far more permanent feature in the garden than flowers, so take as much, if not more, time and care selecting the foliage of plants for the garden**

Leaves come in a remarkable range of shapes, sizes and colours. As we have seen, plants from very hot dry places often have dramatic spiky leaves, or sculpturally succulent ones. Cooler, dry habitats tend to be home to species with very small green leaves or hairy grey leaves. Cold windswept places are populated largely by plants with dense wiry stems clothed in masses of tiny, sometimes scale-like leaves; heathers are a good example. In sheltered, wet environments foliage really takes off, leaves waxing lush on the moisture and fertility.

Often when people design gardens, they plan flower combinations with minute care, and then forget all about the leaves. However, good foliage contrast can keep a garden stimulating for at least half the year. A border with no leaf interest is going to look dull as soon as the flowers finish. At the other extreme, a border that is packed with every leaf shape that it is possible to grow might well look fussy and restless. As is usual with life, there is a happy medium. Just as packing a border with all the colours of the floral palette is rarely as pleasing or successful as limiting the selection to a few, so it tends to be more effective to select a limited, complementary range of foliage hues and forms.

◄ **Their leaves may echo each other, but the leaves of verbascums and blue spruce offer a total contrast in just about every other way.**

ACANTHUS · ARALIA · CROCOSMIA PANICULATA · VERBASCUM

# TEXTURE VARIATION

## AN ADDED DIMENSION IS SURFACE, NOT TO BE UNDERESTIMATED IN ITS IMPACT

The texture of individual leaves can be appreciated close up, by both sight and touch. However, it is the overall visual texture we are concerned with here, how a plant reflects light when seen from the distance.

Glossy leaves reflect light strongly, so much so that a very glossy plant will 'leap out' of a border, in the way that a strong form will act as an 'eyecatcher' or a brightly coloured flower draws attention to itself. All of these, because of their tendency to stand out, have the effect of foreshortening perspective, which can make a garden seem smaller than it really is. So, use glossy leaves carefully. Too many, especially if they are of widely different shapes, can seem overstimulating and tiring. But gloss adds life and sparkle. It also looks permanently fresh; leaves such as those of many hollies, or the bay laurel (*Prunus laurocerasus*), look healthy and full of life. It is the hard surfaces of evergreens such as these that provide the glossiest leaf surfaces.

**The impact a plant makes can be determined by the leaf texture: bright gloss or soothing matt**

While glossy leaves reflect light, those with a matt texture absorb it, and thus 'retire', sinking a little into the background. Having such a plant at the end of the garden or border can actually make it seem further away. But make sure you select something with presence, such as cordyline. It is not just the leaf surface that makes a plant matt rather than glossy, it is also leaf size, small-leaved plants usually appearing matt.

Plants with strong shapes and glossy leaves appear definite and hard. They need softer forms and textures around them if the garden is not to resemble a crowded art gallery. Ferns, chiefly those with intricately divided foliage, are useful counterpoints. Forms of *Polystichum setiferum* are

▲ *Potentilla anserina* and the grass *Milium effusum* 'Aureum' are a wonderful contrast not only in colour but in shape and texture.

**CANNA · DESCHAMPSIA FLEXUOSA · MELIANTHUS MAJOR**

▶ The big, bold exotic foliage of cannas makes them thoroughly architectural, but the pencil-fine variegation of this variety adds another whole dimension.

especially good in this respect. But it is grasses that give us the most attractive soft textures for the border. The two species of deschampsia, *D. caespitosa* and *D. flexuosa*, are among the best. The first gives us the nearest thing to a captive cloud we can have while the second is more of a light mist.

As well as this, there are the useful tools of plants with hairy leaves, such as *Stachys byzantina*, or those with glaucous foliage, such as rue (*Ruta graveolens*), and the often sinister effect of heavily-veined leaves, such as hostas or comfreys. All of these can be used to affect mood as much as to give textural variety.

MILLIUM EFFUSUM 'AUREUM' · POLYSTICHUM · PRUNUS LAUROCERASUS

◄ Complex delicacy alongside simple linearity; a dryopteris fern and *Iris foetidissima*. Both will thrive in shade.

▲ Peonies may be grown primarily for their showy (or blowsy?) flowers, but their young growth, deep-red and fresh with spring vigour, is something to appreciate in its own right.

◀ It is unfair to denounce all rhododendron foliage as funereal and dull. Technically called 'indumentum', the fur on the young foliage of many species has beauty and charm.

▲ Lily-of-the-valley is a groundcover plant for shade which seems the epitome of neatness, never a leaf out of place. Its companion is a copper beech.

▲ Some think bergenias are coarse and clumsy, calling them 'elephants ears', but they are jolly useful low evergreens and a good contrast to bulb foliage.

# FOCUS ON
## FORM
**WITH A FEW STRIKING SILHOUETTES, GIVE ORDER TO A PLANTING SCHEME**

Any border or planting is going to benefit from a few plants that lift the level of interest, holding the eye as it roves across the garden. It is a question of 'changing the pace', breaking up the texture of a mass of more typical leaf shapes. Irises are especially useful in this respect. There is an iris for almost every situation; bearded irises for hot, dry sites, Siberian iris varieties for most garden situations, various bog irises for waterlogged areas, even some, such as the adaptable and evergreen *Iris foetidissima*, for shade. Their sword-shaped leaves or long, thinner strap-like foliage create a strong focal point, particularly in large clumps. Radiating linear leaves also have a strong impact, like those of the day lilies (*Hemerocallis* spp.).

Grasses, bamboos and sedges are also invaluable for their linear leaves and stems that provide interest and variation. More distinctive still are those plants which have a strongly rosette-forming character and linear leaves like phormiums and yuccas, or on a less dramatic scale, the red-hot pokers (*Kniphofia* spp.).

Variation in borders can also be achieved by choosing plants whose leaves are especially large or distinctively shaped. A shrub border can be livened up considerably by the addition of *Hydrangea sargentiana*, with its large leaves, or *Griselinia littoralis*, with its unusual glossy foliage. Perennial plantings can likewise be given a lift with plants like bergenias and hellebores. These are not overly dramatic, but they have quite large, fine, evergreen leaves and a tidy growth pattern that can easily be the focus of attention in the quieter seasons. These are the kind of long-season plants

> **It could be argued that foliage form and shape has more impact on a garden than anything else, especially where the foliage is evergreen**

**FATSIA JAPONICA · GRISELINIA · HEMEROCALLIS · HYDRANGEA**

that we should always be on the look out for when visiting garden centres, if only we can tear ourselves away from the lure of whatever is currently in flower!

Planning with foliage can be taken a stage further. Instead of just adding some distinct foliage for occasional points of contrast, a planting can be designed so that foliage and texture become the key elements, flowers merely extra spice. For example, a sunny dry garden can be planted with broad sweeps of low, mound-forming, sun-loving shrubs like lavenders, cistus and sage. The overall effect will be cohesive, although there will be variations in texture and colour. As a contrast, add sun-loving grasses such as *Stipa gigantea*; their widely spreading but wispy, insubstantial forms will add a lightness of touch. The occasional yucca is also appropriate and forms a good strong contrast.

Really large-leaved plants are arguably at their most effective in splendid isolation, surrounded by their smaller-leaved fellows. *Fatsia japonica*, one of the best hardy, large-leaved shrubs, looks at its finest in simple surroundings, its dark, glossy, hand-shaped leaves complemented only by paler green bamboos and ferns. An exception is where a deliberately tropical effect is being sought, the hurly-burly of contrasting leaf shapes conjuring up the ordered chaos of the rain forest.

Confined spaces are among the most difficult places to plant, especially those around the house, where most of us want something that consistently looks good. Foliage plants really come into their own here. Ferns should always be at the top of the list for consideration in shady spots. They vary tremendously in their foliage, but most, the finely-divided ones especially, benefit from a site that allows close, appreciative inspection. Even something as large (and potentially overpowering) as *Viburnum rhytidophyllum,* an evergreen shrub with leaves 20cm (8in) long and heavily textured and veined, can benefit from planting so that it can be studied close to.

▲ Fine foliage makes a foreground for a view, framed by a gap left in the perimeter planting. The big leaves are *Darmera peltata.*

IRIS FOETIDISSIMA · KNIPHOFIA · STIPA GIGANTEA · VIBURNUM

# EVERGREEN PLANTS
## PERMANENCE AND STRONG FORMS CAPTURED BY THE BEST OF THESE PLANTS

Evergreens have been favourite garden plants since gardening began. Some can be relied upon to stay green through, not only winter, but severe summer droughts too, which accounts for their popularity. Evergreens are architectural, not just because their dark foliage ensures a sense of structure in gardens in the growing season as well as in winter, but also because their unchanging nature helps to develop a sense of permanence and continuity.

However, permanence and popularity both have their flip sides. The very unchanging nature of evergreens can become boring, especially if they are overused. Just as familiarity breeds contempt, so popularity breeds cliché.

The answer to the architectural use of evergreens is to be selective, just a few in key positions or roles to which they are ideally suited, such as permanent hedging. Choose those that develop fine and elegant forms: noble and sculptural pines, narrowly vertical cypress varieties, fine-leaved and naturally symmetrical hollies. If you do not intend to clip regularly, avoid or use carefully, those which grow into vast, ill-defined shapes, such as laurels and the broader-growing cypresses.

▲ *Euphorbia characias* is one of the more reliable and architectural of a rewarding group of plants, adding distinction to the border at all times, but especially in winter.

**Evergreens can be used to punctuate a garden design, ensuring year-round interest and substance**

Beware, too, of the fact that very little will grow under evergreens, though *Euphorbia characias*, *E. robbiae* and the ivies (*Hedera* spp.) can grow at the edge of their shade. For confined spaces, select those with a narrow, columnar growth habit. Fortunately narrow species or forms of many common groups are available. *Picea omorika* is a spruce of classic Christmas tree-shape but which is remarkably narrow, a most striking tree for the smaller garden, or the upright form of the Scots pine (*Pinus sylvestris* 'Fastigiata').

CUPRESSUS · EUCALYPTUS · EUPHORBIA CHARACIAS · HEBE

Most evergreens do have very dark foliage which can make them oppressive, even in the winter when we might welcome any green. However, there are evergreens with a lighter touch; the hebes for instance, smallish shrubs with leaves that are often light green or grey, or even pink tinged. The grey or glaucous leaves of eucalyptus are also a welcome variation on dark green, although the habit of these rapidly growing, sculptural trees is very informal.

Since evergreens are mostly appreciated in winter, they need to be placed so that they can make the maximum impact during this season while still playing a useful part in the warmer months as well. The classic yew hedge is an example of how this works. During the winter its outline is clear and quite dominant; it is often the only thing worth looking at next to the bare soil and dry sticks. In summer its role as a framework is more subtly appreciated, but its role as a backdrop for the colours of the border is vital too.

ILEX · LAVANDULA · PICEA OMORIKA · PINUS · TAXUS BACCATA

# 4 LOCATION & AMBIENCE

It is customary for gardeners to see certain sites and soils as 'problem areas', hot dry banks, shade and poor drainage being three such culprits. What nonsense! The imaginative gardener sees the potential in places such as these, as specialized plant communities can be grown that not only relish the conditions, but look wonderful too.

The key is to explore the plant possibilities that 'problem sites' offer and then to think about the atmosphere that you can conjure up: Mediterranean hillside, woodland, jungle, romantic waterside. Looking to the site to provide inspiration is one way of working with nature. The days when gardeners could blithely ignore the environment are long since gone, days when the advice would have been to plough in peat and chemicals, or drain or irrigate. When creating a garden, nature should not be seen as a constraint, but as a partner.

► A slender juniper makes a focal point in what might otherwise be an amorphous planting, yet it takes up so little ground space.

# THE EXOTIC
## LOOK
### BY IMAGINATIVE SELECTION, THE RAIN FOREST CAN BE BROUGHT TO A CITY GARDEN

Of the differences between tropical and temperate climates, it is the nature of foliage that first strikes the gardener. Tropical leaves tend to be bigger and lusher, with a wider variety of forms. Wherever there is enough light for things to grow, there is an extraordinary range of leaf shapes jostling for attention, a mass of hungry climbers threading their way across trees, shrubs and perennials. Epiphytes like orchids and bromeliads cling to branches and trunks, not because they are parasites, but because they can more easily get the moisture, nutrients and light they need by being attached to another plant.

**An array of sizes, shapes and heights are at the heart of the tropical look, with every nook and space filled**

There are plants, a few very hardy, others hardy in sheltered areas, that can be used to create a tropical ambience. Large leafy plants like gunnera and rodgersia that relish wet conditions (see page 96) are a vital part of this kind of planting, along with tall reedy grasses such as *Arundo donax* and miscanthus species, especially *M. saccharifolius*, the tallest hardy grass. Palms are a must, trachycarpus species being hardy in most areas, *Chamaerops humilis* in sheltered warm spots, and, depending on your climate, you may be lucky with the date palm relative *Phoenix canariensis*, or species of *Butia capitata*.

Anything with unusual foliage is a must, whether it really does look tropical like species of canna and hedychium or is just extraordinary, full stop, such as the monkey puzzle tree (*Araucaria araucana*).

▲ Cannas give a tropical look to wherever they are planted, and do especially well in moist situations. Being tender, they will need lifting or insulating in winter.

ARAUCARIA · ARUNDO · BUTIA CAPITATA · CHAMAEROPS · CLEMATIS ARMANDII

The site for an exotic planting must be out of the wind. However, hardy exotics with smaller or tougher leaves may well tolerate mild, maritime, blustery climates. A warm spot, free from severe frosts, is not vital but it will add considerably to the range of plants that can be grown.

Whether the site is sunny or shaded can have considerable effect on the nature of your tropical paradise. An open sunny area is fine for palms and yuccas, but the rainforest look can also be developed in light shade. Phormiums will tolerate some shade while, for ferns, it is vital. Ferns need both moisture and atmospheric humidity, especially the hardy tree ferns. Climbers are vital, hanging down in swags from branches or walls; large-leaved ones like kiwi fruit (*Actinidia chinensis*) or evergreens like *Clematis armandii* will have the desired effect. Bamboos, too, are jungle plants. Finally, do not forget the epiphytes (non-parasitic plants that grow on other plants). In humid climates, the creeping fern, *Polypodium vulgare*, will happily grow among the moss on branches. Many larger ferns can be persuaded to do so, if transplanted when small. In a very wet climate, some smaller rhododendrons are epiphytes too.

▼ **Hardy plants with tropical-looking foliage are unrivalled for introducing an air of fantasy to the garden. Amongst them one is transported to a tropical paradise.**

# THE SUN-BAKED LOOK

ONCE YOU ACCEPT THE DRY NATURE OF YOUR GARDEN, ALL KINDS OF PLANTING POSSIBILITIES OPEN UP

◄ Gardens in hot, dry climates can become a veritable art gallery of sculptural plants, such as this agave. Even in cooler regions, succulents are best grown out of doors in summer.

Regions that experience regular drought often have a beauty of their own. It is not just the range of grey-greens and subtle browns that plants in such places display, it is their form; rounded hummocks of lavender or heather, sculptural trees such as cork oaks and arbutus, the grace and haze of grasses. Drier and hotter regions can overwhelm with the variety of shapes adopted by succulents.

Sun and good drainage are vital, protection from cold winds preferable, and a poor stony soil may be a positive advantage. The low shrubs typical of these climates often flower spectacularly, but they do need something more architectural to give extra interest. Yuccas are the most striking. Brooms (*Cytisus* and *Genista* spp.), with their twiggy stems, are a good contrast. Herbaceous plants add variation, especially eryngiums, mulleins (*Verbascum* spp.) and the large leafy sea kales. Grasses are also an important source of visual variation.

Drought-tolerant trees often have a distinctive habit. There are many attractive conifers of which the best is probably *Pinus pinea*. But, since trees cast shade, their planting will need to be limited.

**Drought-tolerant plants take on a wealth of leaf shapes and forms. Succulents are the kings of the bizarre, satisfying the most fertile imagination**

Climates where winter frosts are light enable a range of true desert plants to grow. To bring a sense of unity to the extraordinary variety of shapes that succulents take, select one shape, say the rosettes of agaves and yuccas, and then repeat it at selected intervals to create a sense of rhythm throughout the planting. Having created this basic, visual framework it will then be possible to add a wide variety of different shapes, without the whole becoming a muddle. Small, ground cover succulents like lampranthus and sedum are also useful, as they carpet the ground.

**CRAMBE MARITIMA · CYTISUS · PINUS PINEA · VERBASCUM · YUCCA**

# THE JAPANESE LOOK

## ONE OF THE MOST TRULY ARCHITECTURAL STYLES, WHERE FORM PLAYS A VITAL ROLE

The essential elements of Japanese gardens are asymmetry, an appreciation of form and the attempt to capture the essence of natural beauty. They are quite a sensible proposition on acid soils, where growing more luxuriant plants may be unrewarding. Such a soil is ideal for the conifers, maples and water iris, *Iris ensata* (syn. *I. kaempferi*) that are among the important elements of the Japanese garden.

**Harmony is central to the Japanese gardening tradition, which is a sophisticated, clear vision expressed through plants**

Plants for a Japanese garden do not have to be Japanese natives. Those that will look appropriate in a Japanese-style garden include sculptural dwarf conifers, elegant grasses, shrubs and perennials with understated beauty and grace.

It helps, however, to have a few genuinely Japanese plants. Bamboos and maples are the vital references for most people, but the list of readily available Japanese plants includes the pine, *Pinus parviflora* (as seen on willow-pattern china), forms of the cypress *Chamaecyparis pisifera*, and the vigorous climber, *Vitis coignetiae*.

Clipped shrubs are frequently used in traditional Japanese gardens; azaleas, *Ilex crenata*, and *Buxus microphylla* being the preferred plants. Rounded forms often imitating boulders are typical shapes.

To these classic plants may be added the grass *Melica altissima atropurpurea*, or the perennial, *Alchemilla mollis*. Combined with a bridge, a shrine or raked gravel or sand, a true interpretation of Japanese harmony can be created. A Japanese visitor may not be taken in, but most of us need only catch a glimpse of one classic element, such as a stone lantern, to completely absorb the mood.

► Only a few plant varieties are needed in Japanese-style gardens to complement rockwork and a lantern. The strap-shaped leaves are a species of liriope.

**ILEX CRENATA · LIRIOPE · PINUS PARVIFLORA · VITIS COIGNETIAE**

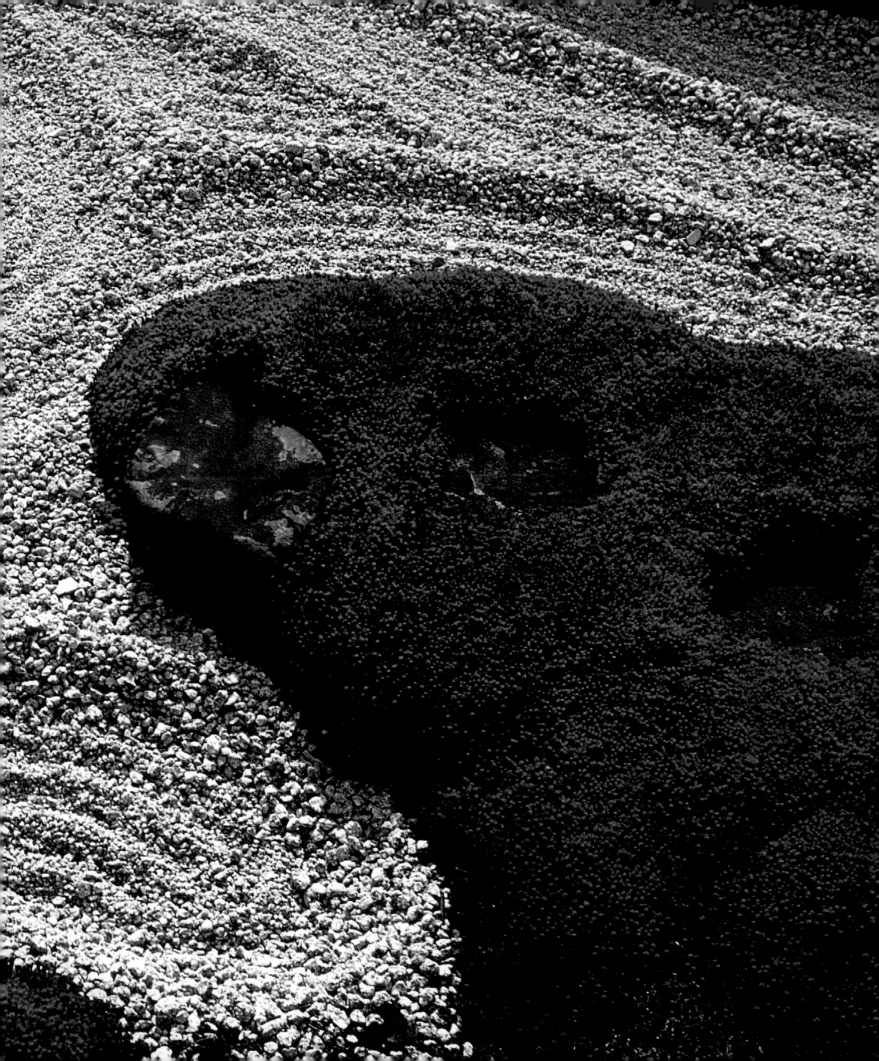

# WATERSIDE EXUBERANCE

## NOTHING MATCHES THE LUSH APPEAL OF WATER-LOVING PLANTS GROWN IN THEIR ELEMENT

The luxuriance of the tropics finds its nearest natural temperate counterpart in fertile wetland habitats. There are few constraints – drought or lack of nutrients – on growth continuing throughout the growing season. While many moisture-loving plants make good leafy architectural plants for ordinary border conditions, they respond so much better with their feet in water.

**Make the most of a damp pond-edge or boggy conditions, adding lush abundance and drama to the garden scene**

Those who live on 'badly drained' soils might consider making the most of this potentially lush situation by planting a selection of the large perennials that will thrive. Those with only a small damp patch or an artificial moist area, perhaps associated with a pond, will have to content themselves with a smaller grouping of plants. Even relatively confined gardens often have a small pond which can be an important and attractive garden feature, starring some good foliage plants, but these should be chosen carefully for size.

Perennials of the magnitude of *Gunnera manicata* or the reed *Arundo donax* are best left to the large garden or the consciously exotic planting (see page 88). While not so big, rampant spreaders like *Petasites japonicus* and *Rodgersia podophylla* are best kept to the larger garden as well. The next size down are those plants with a spread of a metre (3ft) or less, most rodgersias with their brown-tinged spreading leaves, rheums (ornamental rhubarb) and hostas. Most of these leaf shapes are rounded and spreading, so linear contrasts are needed: the yellow flag iris, *Iris pseudacorus*, is a good one, or the arching strap-shaped leaves of the sedge, *Carex pendula*. If your soil is acid, space should be found if possible for the royal fern (*Osmunda*

**CAREX PENDULA · DARMERA PELTATA · IRIS PSEUDACORUS**

*regalis*), perhaps the most architectural waterside plant of all, forming an upright clump of fresh green leaves of somewhat primeval aspect, that looks at its best when rising from above low-growing plants.

The edge of a pond or other body of still water is an important habitat in its own right, with species of a linear upward form predominating, such as water irises, reedmaces (*Typha* spp.) and flowering rush (*Butomus umbellatus*). Those who garden on the edge of a large body of water may indulge themselves with one of the plant world's most romantic sights, a mass of reeds bowing before the breeze. However, the common reed (*Phragmites australis*) is terribly invasive, and in some countries where it is not native its cultivation is banned. A little ingenuity, though, can bring the romance of the reed to smaller bodies of water. The water's edge may be planted with marginal species that do not run wild and the reeds may be evoked by miscanthus grasses planted further back on dry (or drier) land. *Miscanthus sinensis* and its varieties have an elegance that is very close to the real reed.

The very small garden pond or damp patch needs plants that are not going to take over in one summer; smaller hostas, the rounded, glossy leaves of kingcup (*Caltha palustris*) and sedges such as *Carex plantaginea*, with broad, pleated leaves are good choices. Sensibly planted, even a tiny pond or bog garden can contribute both architectural form and exuberant lushness to a garden. It is even possible to plant up a large tub, or a half-barrel with miniature waterside plants.

▼ *Gunnera manicata* is an essential plant in the larger water garden. *Darmera peltata* is a good alternative for the smaller.

GUNNERA MANICATA · OSMUNDA REGALIS · PETASITES · RODGERSIA

▲ The contrast in foliage colour, shape and texture created by these bog-loving plants can be used to great effect in an intimate planting like this one.

▼ Sprawling water plants growing in individual clumps along the edge of the pond accentuate the stillness of the water's surface.

▲ An old stone drinking fountain stands partly concealed by its frame of lush gunnera, ferns and bright pink candelabra primulas, which also lead the eye towards the fountain.

► The unmistakeable leaves of *Gunnera manicata* dominate the foreground of this well-filled water garden. Splashes of colour lead the eye beyond.

▲ The bold reddish foliage of this attractive *Rodgersia pinnata* 'Superba' stands out perfectly against a green background, and is particularly useful in a semi-shaded site.

# WOODLAND GARDEN
## DAPPLED SHADE OR DEEP SHADOW, BOTH HAVE NATURAL ALLIES

Woodlands can be magical places, ferns and other luxuriant green plants covering the ground, running among the dead leaves of the previous autumn and the rotting remains of fallen trees. Because light levels in deciduous woods are at their highest in late winter and early spring before the trees grow leaves, this is the time when the majority of woodland plants flower. Many grow from bulbs and tubers, retreating below ground as light levels fall with the onset of summer and leaf. Other woodland plants tend to be evergreens, with dark leaves that can extract every bit of sunlight at all times of the year. These evergreens provide much of the excitement of woodland gardening.

**Do not feel defeated by shade; even the most challenging situations will satisfy some remarkably determined plants**

Shaded gardens come in many forms. Those with the most potential are lightly shaded, with a moist soil. Here there is no problem in growing a wide range of plants, and it is possible to generate a feeling of lushness with a generous display of ferns, from large dryopteris and polystichum to small creeping thelypteris and polypodium. Broader-leaved flowering plants can be used for contrast: hostas, the elegant solomon's seals (*Polygonatum* and *Smilacina* spp.), arums, astilbes and arisaemas. Bamboos will flourish if the shade is not too heavy, contributing height and the grace of their bending canes.

Deeper shade restricts what can be grown, especially if it is beneath trees such as beech and maple that carpet the ground heavily with leaves in autumn and take out a lot of nutrients and moisture. Further problems are created if the soil is dry for much of the year, as dry shade is one of the most problematic areas in the garden. However, there are plants that will survive

▶ A shady dell with a stream running through it is a heaven-sent opportunity for exuberant plantings of large ferns and other moisture loving plants.

ARUNCUS · ASTILBE · DRYOPTERIS · POLYGONATUM

◄ The soft light levels of woodland create a magical atmosphere, here enhanced by over-hanging foliage and a curving wooden pathway, leading off into the trees.

and grow even in these inhospitable conditions, including some very good architectural ones. Male fern (*Dryopteris filix-mas*), the majestic dark mound of *Helleborus foetidus* and the large sedge, *Carex pendula*, which has catkin-like flowers hanging from arching stems, will do much to improve matters. Certain euphorbias are worth trying, *E. characias* and the creeping *E. robbiae* especially. In the very worst places, ivies (notably *Hedera helix*), and possibly periwinkles (*Vinca* spp.), are about the only things that will grow.

While few grasses survive in shade, there are some that will – the broad-bladed species of melica, for instance. Better still, though, are sedges and woodrushes, the *Luzula* species. The latter will cope with dry shade, although on better soils they form an interesting evergreen ground cover of coarse grassy leaves more quickly. They, and shade tolerant plants like the creeping dead nettles (*Lamium* and *Galeobdolon* spp.) and periwinkles, can be used to cover extensive areas of ground in shade with a good architectural contrast provided by occasional larger and more upright plants; dryopteris ferns, for example.

▲ There is no denying the value of hostas in shady or moist gardens. They are best mixed with other plants such as ferns, or, as here, *Arum italicum* 'Pictum'.

The most problematic areas of shade are those where the gardener has to deal not with nature but with the legacy of human interference. The sunless sides of houses, where the soil is impoverished by large amounts of rubble, are

**Punctuate a carpet of shade-loving plants with an occasional surprise – an upright fern amongst low-growing creepers**

probably the worst. This is bad news for woodland plants as the most desirable ones always seem to need a moist soil, rich in organic matter. The plants most likely to cope are those recommended for dry shade. The alternative is to improve the soil by introducing plenty of organic matter such as garden compost, manure, rotted straw, or even seaweed, which in coastal areas can make quite an attractive, healthy mulch.

HEDERA HELIX · HELLEBORUS FOETIDUS · HOSTA · VINCA

# PLANT DIRECTORY

Choosing which plants to include or leave out of a list of architectural plants is difficult, especially since definitions of what is architectural vary. What follows is intended to be a guide to the most commonly available plants, the most useful architecturally, and some which are highly distinctive, but might need to be sought out in the catalogues of specialist nurseries.

Plants are divided into groups: trees and shrubs, climbers, perennials, ferns and grasses. Sometimes a whole genus, a group of directly related plants, is discussed (for example, arbutus), at other times particular species that are part of a genus (*Acer palmatum*). Varieties, called cultivars if they have been specially bred, are a further sub-division, indicated by a name in single quotation marks (*Corylus avellana* 'Contorta'). Hybrids, created when two different plants are crossed, include a multiplication sign in the name.

The entries focus on the features that reflect the plant's architectural interest. Sizes given mean something slightly different for each category of plants. For the trees, shrubs and climbers, I have given the maximum height x spread, that can be expected in favourable conditions. These dimensions may take many years to achieve. Woody plants in pots are effectively 'bonsai-ed' and will often never achieve their maximum size. Perennials, ferns and grasses are given their height when in flower, which can add to their scale. The spread given represents two or three years' growth in favourable conditions. If plants can be very invasive, this is mentioned.

Hardiness ratings, which follow each entry, break down thus (average minimum temperature given in brackets): Very hardy – hardy in regions with very severe climates (-23°C); Fully hardy – hardy in temperate areas (-17°C); Slightly tender – hardy in most areas but need careful siting, tend to flourish in warm, sheltered sites (-12°C); Tender – hardy only in mild climates but, with winter protection, could be worth trying elsewhere (-1°C).

▶ **Wonderful contrast in foliage shape and colour. Delicate-leaved *Dicentra* is interrupted by the fronds of a fresh green fern.**

# CLIMBERS

## ACTINIDIA CHINENSIS
## (SYN. A. DELICIOSA)
### Chinese gooseberry; kiwi fruit

The source of kiwi fruit is an extravagantly large vine that eventually becomes woody, with exotically large, rounded, hairy leaves. To develop properly it needs either a large expanse of wall or a large tree to climb up. The edible brown-skinned fruits are borne by female plants and only if there is a male nearby to fertilize it. Tolerant of most soils.

**Deciduous twining climber**

**10 x 10m (33 x 33ft); Fully hardy**

## AMPELOPSIS BREVIPEDUNCULATA

An attractive, leafy climber with unusual blue-green fruit and good, yellow or orange autumn colour. There is also a fine, but much more slow-growing variegated form, 'Elegans'. Thrives on most reasonable soils and tolerates some shade.

**Deciduous climber with tendrils**

**5 x 5m (16 x 16ft); Fully hardy**

## ARISTOLOCHIA MACROPHYLLA

A large-leaved climber for generous, sunny spaces, it has the additional delight of yellow- spotted flowers, shaped like bent funnels. Needs shelter from wind and a soil that never dries out if it is to give of its best.

**Deciduous climber with tendrils**

**6 x 6m (20 x 20ft); Fully hardy**

## CLEMATIS ARMANDII

This wonderful plant is practically the only one to have both good flowers (white or blush pink, in late spring) and oval evergreen leaves. An invaluable plant for

*Actinidia chinensis*

the tropical look. Vigorous and hardy, it must still be kept out of cold winds. Moist but well drained soils are needed, with shade for the roots, sun for the crown.

**Evergreen twining climber**

**7 x 7m (23 x 23ft); Fully hardy**

## × FATSHEDERA LIZEI

A hybrid between *Fatsia japonica* and *Hedera helix* (the common or English ivy), hence the 'x'. It forms a pretty messy mound if left to its own devices, but if trained as a climber, either on a wall or on a free-

*Clematis armandii*

standing support, it looks distinguished. The leaves are dark green and ivy-like, the flowers, which appear in late autumn, are creamy-white. Can grow on any reasonably fertile soil, in sun or shade.

**Evergreen shrub or climber**

**1.5 x 2m (5 x 6½ft); Fully hardy**

## HEDERA
### Ivy

Ivies are among the most useful of climbers – for being evergreen, fast-growing once established and for their habit of self-clinging, making the trellis or wires needed by most climbers unnecessary. Contrary to popular opinion, ivies neither kill trees nor damage houses. Indeed, the plants' ability to climb, unaided, up brickwork makes them invaluable for hiding large expanses of unattractive wall. Their winter flowers are an important wildlife resource, as are their berries, while their dense growth is an important sheltering place for a variety of insects and birds.

Ivies are not fussy about soil and flourish in quite deep shade as well as in sunlight. Once established and growing fast, they may well need decisive pruning to keep them from becoming too large.

The common or English ivy, *H. helix*, is not to be despised, despite its ubiquity. Its hardiness and adaptability make it one of the mainstays of the garden, while the enormous number of varieties, many with gold or cream variegations, ensures that there is always an ivy for every place. Do some research before you buy, however, as the varieties do tend to vary in hardiness and shade tolerance. *H. canariensis* is somewhat more exotic-looking than the common ivy, with its large, slightly floppy-

*Hedera canariensis* 'Gloire de marengo'

looking leaves, and is available in a number of varieties, many of them with cream variegations, such as 'Gloire de Marengo'. Dislikes cold wind.

**Evergreen self-clinging climbers**

**6–10 x 5m (20–33 x 5ft); Fully to very hardy**

## HYDRANGEA PETIOLARIS
## (H. ANOMALA SUBSP. PETIOLARIS)
### Climbing hydrangea

In the manner of ivy (see previous entry), this hydrangea climbs by means of aerial roots that cling to its support, which makes it very useful for covering large expanses of bare wall, although it is only fair to point out that it will take many years to do so. It has robust, green serrated leaves and, on established plants, small white flower heads in summer. Being shade tolerant, it is useful for clothing sunless walls. A relatively unfussy plant, climbing hydrangea will grow in most soils – ideally, ones that are moist but well-drained.

**Deciduous self-clinging climber**

**20 x 15m (60 x 50ft); Fully hardy**

## LAPAGERIA ROSEA
### Chilean bellflower; copihue

The Chilean national flower, this is arguably one of the most beautiful of all flowering plants. Its dark green oval leaves have a tropical feel to them, enhanced when the elegantly pendant, thick, waxy, pinky-red, bell-shaped flowers emerge from summer to late autumn. The Chilean bellflower makes an ideal plant for the cool, partly shaded conservatory, or for sheltered and lightly shaded spots outside. Extremes of heat and cold have to be avoided, as does wind. Best on an acid soil.

**Evergreen twining climber**

**3 x 2m (10 x 6½ft); Slightly tender**

*Vitis coignetiae*

*Parthenocissus henryana*

## MUEHLENBECKIA COMPLEXIA
### Maidenhair creeper

This New Zealand native has tiny leaves on dark wiry stems; these stems climb up anything they can attach themselves to. It makes a useful trailer to bundle over walls or a climber to hide chicken wire. It is used in some parts of the world as a subject for topiary, being trained over shaped mesh and then trimmed. As a fast-grower, it would need fairly frequent hair cuts! It produces tiny off-white flowers in mid-summer, followed by waxy white berries. Not suitable for severe continental climates, while it can spread to nuisance proportions in mild maritime ones if not kept in check. Suitable for most soils.

**Deciduous shrub or twining climber**
**3 x 3m (10 x 10ft); Slightly tender**

## PARTHENOCISSUS
### Virginia creeper

These climbers always look good on a building, adding a patina of age and distinction. Like ivy, it is self-clinging, in this case by means of tendrils. The true Virginia creeper is *P. quinquefolia*; *P. tricuspidata* is similar and *P. henryana* is somewhat smaller and has distinct white veins in the middle of the leaflets. Fiery autumn colour is another of their merits. While they are normally grown on buildings, do not forget their natural way of growing, in trees. Cultivated like this, with great swags of growth hanging down from upper branches, they recreate the luxuriant feeling of a tropical jungle. All flourish in good, moist soils, making rapid growth in either sun or shade.

**Deciduous self-clinging climbers**
**6–10 x 6–10m (20–33 x 20–33ft);**
**Very hardy**

## VITIS COIGNETIAE
### Crimson glory vine

One of the classic subjects for Japanese painters, this vine combines elegance with strength. A vast and vigorous climber, it is best used to grow over trees or buildings. The handsome, well-veined leaves turn rich reds and oranges in autumn. Inedible, dark fruit is occasionally borne. Grows in full sun or part shade and in most reasonable soils.

**Deciduous climber with tendrils**
**12 x 12m (40 x 40ft); Fully hardy**

# FERNS

## ASPLENIUM SCOLOPENDRIUM
### (PHYLLITIS SCOLOPENDRIUM)

Possibly the most shade-tolerant of any plant worth growing, its fresh green strap-like fronds are a godsend in the dark spots. Its form and colour make it an invaluable contrast to other ferns and shade-loving plants. There are a number of named forms with wavy-edged fronds (which look like seaweed) or divided ones. Use in any soils that do not suffer summer drought.

**Evergreen fern**

**30 x 30cm (12 x 2in); Very hardy**

## BLECHNUM CHILENSE

An exceptionally good fern for damp spots in mild climates, with that primeval look that seems to be just waiting for a brontosaurus! Its relatively undivided fronds thrust up from a spreading rootstock, eventually forming large tough mats.

**Evergreen fern**

**75 x 75cm (2½ x 2½ft); Slightly tender**

## DICKSONIA ANTARCTICA
### Australian tree fern

This tree fern is really primeval. Roughly like a palm in form, with a head of huge fronds atop a fibrous trunk, it transforms pedestrian shade into rain forest. It is hardy in light to medium frosts but must have humidity as the trunk absorbs moisture rather than the roots which are there mainly for stability. This unfortunately restricts its use as a garden plant to areas of high and regular rainfall. Some shade is a must.

**Evergreen fern**

**3 x 3m (10 x 10ft); Tender to slightly tender**

## DRYOPTERIS

A varied genus of ferns, all with the same distinct vase shape as the fronds grow from a single central point. *D. filix-mas*, the male fern, is rather dull, but very valuable as it is evergreen in mild winters and is one of the best ferns for dry shade. *D. pseudomas* is an improved form and also pretty adaptable. *D. erythrosora* has lovely, tan brown young growth turning to glossy green. *D. cycadina* and *D. wallichiana* are rather magnificent, with very neatly arranged growth, while *D. dilatata* spreads wide and is of lush appearance to be grown in particularly moist shade. Most reasonable soils and shade will suit the plants.

**Deciduous ferns**

**60–100 x 60–100cm (2–3 x 2–3ft); Fully hardy**

## MATTEUCCIA STRUTHIOPTERIS

A neatly erect shuttlecock of fresh green fronds make this a particularly desirable fern. Needs moist soil and shelter from wind.

**Deciduous rhizomatous fern**

**100 x 60cm (3 x 2ft); Very hardy**

## OSMUNDA REGALIS
### Royal fern

Once established in the acid, moist conditions it likes, this is one of the most majestic of ferns, or even of all hardy perennials. Its broad, relatively undivided fronds and upright habit give it a real presence in the landscape. Strange brown fronds grow upright in the centre of the plant during the summer; these are spore bearing. It will tolerate sun.

**Deciduous fern**

**1.2 x 1m (4 x 3ft); Very hardy**

*Dicksonia antarctica*

*Dryopteris filix-mas*

## POLYPODIUM VULGARE
### Polypody

An intriguing fern of creeping habit, and there are various forms available with more elaborately cut fronds. In nature, it tends to grow on mossy tree trunks, at least in wet climates, and may be encouraged to do so on trees in the garden. Otherwise, it is a good loose ground cover in moist, shady places.

**Evergreen rhizomatous fern**
**20 x 30cm (8 x 12in); Very hardy**

## POLYSTICHUM

Many of these species are useful garden plants, not only handsome, but more tolerant of dry shade than most ferns.

Of these evergreen ferns, the fully hardy *P. acrostichoides*, or Christmas fern, up to 60 x 60cm (2 x 2ft), has an ability to cope with dry shade and a reliably evergreen habit which make it a very desirable plant despite the fact that the fronds are not as daintily divided as we might wish.

*P. munitum*, the giant holly fern, 1 x 1m (3 x 3ft), is a magnificent and luxuriant evergreen fern with finely cut fronds in a good dark green. *P. aculeatum* is smaller.

### *P. setiferum*
### Soft shield fern

A gardener's dream: beautifully divided foliage, evergreen except in severe winters, reasonably tolerant of dry shade and sun, and easily obtained. It comes in several different forms which vary in the level of division of the foliage and considerably in size. *P. s.* 'Acutilobum' is one of the best.

**Evergreen or semi-evergreen fern**
**30–100 x 30–75cm (1–3 x 1–2½ft);**
**Very to fully hardy**

*Polystichum setiferum*

# GRASSES

## ARUNDO DONAX
### Giant reed

Familiar in warm climates, this grass is reasonably hardy, if slower growing, elsewhere. It has greyish leaves which can get very tatty with age, but can always be cut down at the end of the year. There is a lovely variegated form but it is not very hardy. Suitable for any reasonably moist soil, the wetter the better. Prefers sun.

**Evergreen grass**

**3 x 1m (10 x 3ft); Fully hardy**

## BAMBOO

Bamboo lovers may regard lumping them all together as tantamount to blasphemy, but to the rest of us they do look remarkably similar, a situation not helped by botanists who seem to change the names annually. These wonderfully elegant plants deserve to be much more widely grown and not just in an oriental context. A visit to a specialist nursery will enable you to appreciate the subtle differences between species.

Bamboos have a reputation for invasiveness, which is not entirely undeserved. Some are, but most are not. Of those that are, *Arundinaria anceps*, 3m (10ft), is as graceful as it is vigorous, with masses of small leaves. Species of pleioblastus and sasa are notorious spreaders; *P. pygmaeus*, 75cm (30in), is small but forms a useful carpet; *S. veitchii* 1.5m (5ft), forms a thicket and develops a dry grey-brown edge to the leaf in the latter part of the year, which some find attractive.

*Semiarundinaria fastuosa*, 3 x 1m (10 x 3ft), is a tall-growing, elegantly vertical bamboo which spreads only slowly.

*Phyllostachys* includes some of the most beautiful bamboos, and they are compact. *P. nigra*, 2.5m x 75cm (8 x 2½ft), is the famous, stylish (and expensive) black-stemmed bamboo. *Chusquea culeou*, 6m x 75cm (20 x 2½ft), is also expensive but it is a very fine, elegant clump-former with small leaves.

*Shibatea kumasasa*, 1.2m x 75cm (4 x 2½ft), is unusual, having small but broad leaves and is well behaved; it makes a useful contrast to the other bamboos. *Indocalamus tessellatus*, 1.5m (5ft), is a very shade-tolerant species with especially broad leaves and is helpful in developing the tropical look. It also grows fast.

All bamboos should be protected from the wind and from drying out in summer. Sun or light shade and good, fertile, moist soils will give the best results.

## CALAMAGROSTIS ×
## ACUTIFLORA
## 'KARL FOERSTER'

A highly distinctive grass whose seed heads stay bolt upright. Thus, a perfect reminder of the vertical in those plantings which may look very colourful late in the summer but are getting messy. It is best not to detract from its special quality by planting anything next to it that approaches it in height. Needs full sun, but any soil is suitable.

**Deciduous grass**

**150 x 30cm (5 x 1ft); Very hardy**

## CAREX
### Sedge

Sedges are a varied and versatile group whose value has only recently been recognized by gardeners. It is their foliage rather than their flowers or seed heads that is the attraction. In general, they are rather more tolerant of poor soils and harsh environments than grasses. These are only the best evergreen perennials:

*C. muskingumensis*, reaching 75 x 40cm (30 x 16in), is unusual in that it grows from the top of the stem rather than the base, as is the case with nearly all other sedges. Fresh green leaves and a slowly spreading habit are typical. Grows in most soils, sun or part shade. *C. pendula*, 1 x 1m (3 x 3ft), has large robust tufts of dark green leaves which are complemented from mid-summer on by long, catkin-like flower heads; these are an unusual and elegant feature, dangling from arching stems. Unfortunately it scatters self-sown seedlings all over the garden. Flourishes in sun or shade, including dry shade. *C. testacea*, growing to 40 x 30cm (16

*Carex elata* 'Aurea'

*Cortaderia selloana*

*Miscanthus sinensis*

x 12in), is the best of the New Zealand sedges, and they are all good. It produces neat clumps of orange-brown leaves that really glow in winter sunshine. Sun and moist soils are best.

**Very to fully hardy**

## CORTADERIA SELLOANA
### Pampas grass

The pampas grass is a noble plant ruined by unimaginative overplanting. It either sits cramped on tiny suburban lawns or stands forlornly on ill-conceived industrial estates. It should be possible to rehabilitate it; perhaps by using its massive bulk of green leaves and waving white plumes only in majestic settings, or only *en masse*. Suits any type of reasonable soil in sun.

The variety *C. selloana* 'Aureo-lineata' has attractively yellow-striped leaves, whilst the variety 'Pumila' is a dwarf form, up to 1.5m (40in), useful for smaller gardens.

**Evergreen grass**

**3 x 2m (10 x 6½ft); Very hardy**

*Deschampsia caespitosa*

## DESCHAMPSIA CAESPITOSA
### Tufted hair grass

A dense clump of foliage produces wonderfully soft heads of flowers and seed throughout the summer, quite unrivalled for soft-focus texture. 'Bronzeschleier' is bronzy, 'Goldschleier' is yellow and quite tall, 'Goldtau' is smaller and golden. Any soil suitable, although acid ones preferred. Grow in sun or part-shade.

**Evergreen grass**

**75 x 50cm (30 x 20in); Very hardy**

## LUZULA
### Woodrush

Broad-leaved grassy plants, good examples are *L. nivea* and *L. sylvatica*. Both are around 60 x 30cm (24 x 12in), the former with creamy flowers and narrow foliage, the latter with brown flowers and broad leaves. Both form ground covering clumps and are happy in sun or shade, tolerating dry shade.

**Evergreen perennials; Very hardy**

## MISCANTHUS

Magnificent grasses for a wide range of uses in the garden. All require fertile moist soils to do well. Of the herbaceous rhizomatous grasses, *M. sacchariofolius*, 2.5 x 1m (8 x 3ft), is one of the tallest hardy species and very useful for creating temporary summer height or a tropical effect.

### *M. sinensis*

This has become one of the most widely used grasses in modern landscape design. It has far more elegance than the over-used pampas grass and, being fully herbaceous, it is a feature of the garden for only part of the year, summer to late winter, so you will not tire of it. Tidy enough for conventional borders, yet natural enough for wild gardens, it has endless possibilities. While the tight clumps of narrow leaves are quite attractive, it is the silvery flower heads blowing in the breeze that give it real character. There are now a large number of varieties, and likely to be more in the future. 'Silberfeder' is the best known, a reliable flowerer with silver-pink heads; 'Zebrinus' has an unusual pattern of variegation with yellow bands across the leaves; 'Gracillimus' is a slightly smaller and daintier form; 'Nippon' and 'Kleine Fontana' are smaller.

**Herbaceous rhizomatous grass**

**2m x 75cm (6½ x 2½ft); Very hardy**

## MOLINIA CAERULEA
### Purple moor grass

This grass forms a tight clump of foliage that sends narrow leaves and wispy flower heads out in all directions. The ordinary form has dark, slightly purple stems, while 'Variegata' has cream variegations. There are other varieties, differing in height and form. All fade to an attractive dry, pale yellow in winter. A remarkably tolerant, tough plant.

**Herbaceous grass**

**1m x 60cm (3 x 2ft); Very hardy**

## PENNISETUM

Inconspicuous or downright dull until they flower, pennisetums make up for lost time by producing mounds of bottle-brush flower heads in mid-summer. Quite unlike the blooms of any other grass in its softness, it is a perfect companion for lavenders, catmint, oreganums and other plants that flourish in

dryish sunny places. *P. villosum* is grey in its overall effect, *P. alopecuroides* and *P. orientale* dull purple. They are hardy in cold continental climates where there is little winter damp but suffer from the combination of wet and cold in maritime ones. Best to grow them hard, on poor, sharply drained soils.

**Deciduous grasses**

**60–75cm x 1m (2–2½ x 3ft); Fully hardy**

## SPODIOPOGON SIBIRICUS

Upright growth, broad leaves and reddish flower panicles make this a good feature grass for late summer and autumn. Succeeds in sun or shade and any good soil.

**Deciduous grass**

**120 x 40cm (4ft x 16in); Fully hardy**

*Stipa gigantea*

## STIPA ARUNDINACEA
### Pheasant grass

Clumps of olive green leaves turn golden brown in winter. It is at its best then and, along with *Carex testacea*, complements evergreens beautifully.

**Evergreen perennial grass**

**60 x 75cm (2 x 2½ft); Slightly tender**

### *S. gigantea*
### Golden oats

From early summer on, this grass bears vast open sprays of oat-like flowers and seeds, an unusual combination of the sizeable and the ethereal. Needs space to look its best. Grow in full sun and light, well-drained soils.

**Deciduous perennial grass**

**1.5 x 1.2m (5 x 4ft); Slightly tender**

# PERENNIALS

## ACANTHUS

It was the ancient Greeks who first immortalized these plants, carving their leaves in stone on their buildings. The leaves are dark glossy green and lobed, the flowers consist of strange spires of hooded mauve-pink foxglove-shaped blooms. *A. latifolius* is the common form, flowering more freely and spreading fearsomely in warm climates. *A. spinosus* is finer and flowers more abundantly than *A. latifolius*. Requires fertile soils in sunny places.

**Herbaceous perennial**

**1.2 x 1m (4 x 3ft); Very hardy**

## AGAVE

Among the most common and characteristic plants of warm climates with dry summers, agaves are supremely architectural. Even if you cannot grow them outside, their aggressively spiky rosettes make splendid and long-lived pot plants, to be brought into a cool light room or greenhouse over the winter. They can also be planted out temporarily in the border. *A. americana* is the most common, with several good variegated forms.

**Evergreen succulent perennials**

**2 x 2m (6½ x 6½ft); Tender**

## ALCHEMILLA MOLLIS

A spreading perennial, with lime-green flowers in early summer and the most beautiful scallop-shaped leaves that trap and roll drops of water like silver globules of mercury. Thrives anywhere that is not too dry, in sun or light shade.

**Herbaceous perennial**

**40 x 75cm (16 x 30in); Very hardy**

*Acanthus spinosus*

## ARALIA

Fortunately becoming more common, these are massive and dramatic perennials that look very exotic. Large hand-shaped leaves, creamy flower heads and dark berries are its prized characteristics. There are a number of similar species: *A. cachmeriana*; *A. californica*; *A. racemosa*. Easy to grow in sun or light shade, in soil that is not too dry.

**Herbaceous perennials**

**2 x 2m (6½ x 6½ft); Very to fully hardy**

## ARISAEMA

These are strange and wonderful members of the arum family, with the usual hooded arum flowers, but in murky colours. The foliage of most species is very attractive and usually three-lobed. *A. triphylla* is a small but vigorous species, forming excellent ground cover in cool shade.

**Tuberous herbaceous perennials**

**30 x 30cm (1 x 1ft); Very hardy**

## ARUNCUS DIOICUS

While most large perennials have the attraction of elephants – that is, impressive, fascinating, but lacking utterly in grace –

this is an exception. Its divided foliage is most elegant, and it forms an attractive upright clump that does not spread too vigorously. Fluffy creamy flower spikes appear in summer. Suitable for sun or shade and any soils, but moister ones are favoured.

**Herbaceous perennial**

**1.8 x 1m (6 x 3ft); Very hardy**

## ASARUM
### Wild ginger

Quiet little plants, almost like vegetable mice that scurry across shady ground. The leaves are a rounded, broad heart-shape, glossy green in the more common varieties such as *A. europaeum*. Others, such as *A. hartwegii*, are so intricately marked with grey and silver that they have become collectors' plants in Japan. Require humus-rich soil in shade.

**Evergreen perennials**

**15 x 30cm (6 x 12in); Very hardy**

## ASPARAGUS OFFICINALIS
### Asparagus

Not just a gourmet's delight but a first-class foliage plant, a vast, upright, thrusting mound of feathery, light green leaves that is a perfect textural element in the border. Best in rich soil in full sun.

**Herbaceous perennial**

**1 x 1m (3 x 3ft); Very hardy**

## ASTILBE RIVULARIS

Usually grown for their flowers, astilbes have quite attractive divided foliage. This one has dull greeny flowers but especially handsome leaves. Suitable for most soils, in sun or light shade.

**Herbaceous perennial**

**1.8 x 1m (6 x 3ft); Fully hardy**

## BAPTISIA AUSTRALIS

Indigo pea flowers are the perfect complement to the neat clump of blue-green leaves of this prairie perennial. There are several other attractive species with white flowers such as *B. leucophaea*. Needs full sun and fertile soil. Once planted it should not be moved.

**Herbaceous perennial**

**100 x 50cm (3ft x 20in); Very hardy**

## BERGENIA
### Elephant's ears

Popular with gardeners for their very early white or pink flowers, the large number of bergenia varieties are first class foliage plants too, their tight mats of glossy, leathery round leaves having earned them their common name. In winter the leaves turn reddish. *B. ciliata* has the finest leaves, more matt than the others, covered in fine hairs. Grows in any soil, sun or semi-shade.

**Evergreen perennials**

**30 x 30–60cm (1 x 1–2ft); Very hardy**

## CANNA

Very tropical in appearance, the cannas are a mainstay of exotic summer bedding schemes where their bright orange, red and yellow flowers shriek for attention. Their broad leaves wrapped around upright stems are a must for the exotic look. *C. iridiflora* has some of the finest foliage, and attractive pink flowers; *C. musifolia*, while not frost hardy, has the most luxuriant foliage. They need rich soil in full sun and winter protection for the rhizomes, with storage indoors in cold areas.

**Rhizomatous herbaceous perennials**

**120 x 60cm (4 x 2ft);**

**Slightly tender to tender**

## CRAMBE
### Sea kale

Large green leaves are rare in dry, infertile habitats, making the crambes valuable plants for such conditions. Their flowers are spectacular, huge clouds of tiny white blooms held well above the leaves. *C. maritima*, the sea kale, up to 60 x 60cm (2 x 2ft), is the smallest and has wonderfully glaucous foliage; *C. cordifolia* and *C. orientalis* are larger, reaching 1.5 x 1m (5 x 3ft).

**Herbaceous perennials and annuals**

**Fully to very hardy**

## CROCOSMIA

Upright linear leaves are always useful for introducing some variation into plantings. The crocosmias form clumps in mild areas, flowering yellow, red or orange in late summer. *C. paniculata* is especially striking, being taller than most, with sword-like leaves of a pleated appearance and clusters of scarlet flowers. Most useful for bringing some sense of order to untidy late season borders. They need full sun in any soil. *C. masonorum* is the most vigorous species.

**Herbaceous perennials**

**60–100 x 30cm (2–3 x 1ft); Fully hardy**

*Crocosmia 'Lucifer'*

## CYNARA CARDUNCULUS
### Cardoon

Primarily known as the cardoon of the gourmet table, this versatile plant doubles as a magnificent ornamental perennial. Large silver, deeply divided and jaggedly-toothed leaves arch out of the ground, eventually producing large, purple thistle-like flower heads atop a thick stem. The vegetable globe artichoke is similar in appearance, but less glaucous. Being vigorous plants, cynara need fertile soil and a warm spot in full sun.

**Herbaceous perennial**

**2.5 x 2m (8 x 6½ft); Very hardy**

*Cynara cardunculus*

*Eryngium giganteum*

## DARMERA PELTATA
### (SYN. PELTIPHYLLUM PELTATUM)

Before any sign of the leaves, the flower stems burst forth great pink heads that appear to grow straight out of the mud in which this plant wallows. The leaves are round, up to 30cm (1ft) across and a fine companion to other lusty waterside plants. Its spreading roots are very useful for erosion control. Grow in sun or shade.

**Herbaceous perennial**

**100 x 60cm (3 x 2ft); Very hardy**

## ECHINOPS RITRO
### Globe thistle

The common name of this plant is an accurate description, for these are robust thistly perennials with tight, blue spherical flower heads in late summer, very good for contrasting with the hazy heads of plants like macleaya or the upright spikes of veronicastrum. Suitable for any soils, including poor ones, and full sun.

**Herbaceous perennial**

**150 x 60cm (5 x 2ft); Very hardy**

## ECHIUM PININIANA

Definitely a plant for the extraterrestrial look, this plant takes several years to grow its large rosettes of long, hairy leaves and then throws forth a towering flower spike carrying thousands and thousands of tiny blue flowers. The whole then dies, leaving a spectacular carcase and masses of seedlings. One of the best tall plants for the garden, but do not expect it to stand up straight! There are several similar species from its native Canary Islands. Grow in full sun and sharp drainage, in mild areas only.

**Evergreen perennial**

**2.5m x 75cm (8 x 2½ft); Tender**

## ERYNGIUM

'Up-market thistles' might be a good description of these highly distinctive perennials, although they are not related to the thistle. They have spiny leaves and the flower heads are set off by collars of bracts. The whole plant can be blue, silver or green and presents a striking architectural spectacle. They are tolerant of a wide range of soils, but most need good drainage. The smaller species are especially valuable for dry, poor soils. Best in sun.

**Herbaceous perennials and biennials**

### *E. agavifolium*

It is the leaves that really make you stop and look at this species, a bold, practically evergreen clump of fresh green straps that elegantly taper to a point, with jagged teeth at the edges. Flowers are rather squat green lumps on stout stems.

**Herbaceous perennial**

**150 x 75cm (5 x 2½ft); Fully hardy**

### *E. giganteum*
### Miss Wilmott's Ghost

This eryngium is biennial, dying after flowering, but it leaves a legacy of seed for future years. The pale grey 'thistles' look almost as good in death as in life. The common name comes from the English gardener who surreptitiously scattered seed around all the gardens she visited!

**Biennial or short-lived perennial**

**100 x 40cm (3ft x 16in); Very hardy**

## EUPATORIUM PURPUREUM
### Joe Pye weed

One of the most imposing of perennials, this is one of several very similar species known as Joe Pye weed in their native eastern North America. It flowers from late summer to early autumn, the shrub-like bulk making its presence keenly felt into the winter. Yet being herbaceous it is low enough to ignore for the rest of the year. Definitely a plant of majesty rather than elegance, as a bonus, its soft pink flowers, held on pinkish stems, attract and feed enormous numbers of butterflies. Best on moister and fertile soils, it needs full sun.

**Herbaceous perennial**

**2.5 x 1m (8 x 3ft); Very hardy**

## EUPHORBIA
### Milkweed; spurge

Euphorbia is one of the most useful architectural plant genera. Beloved by those who regard themselves as horticulturally sophisticated, and who thus appreciate green flowers (here massed in heads of cup-shaped bracts) and elegant foliage, they are regarded with a certain amount of apprehension by those who like their flowers bright. But even the greatest lover of colour must appreciate just how adaptable many of them are, thriving in the conditions that many plants find intolerable. Irritant milky sap makes them usefully unpalatable to animals too.

**Annuals, biennials, perennials;**
**deciduous and evergreen shrubs**

### E. amygdaloides subsp. robbiae

So rapidly spreading that it should not perhaps be grown in the sunny border but kept to dry shade where its invasive tendencies are often a blessing, this euphorbia has dark green leaves and light green-yellow flowers in late winter/early spring. Very useful for filling awkward gaps.

**Evergreen perennial**
**40 x 60cm (16 x 24in); Fully hardy**

### E. characias

Neatly shrubby in shape, this is one of the most useful winter plants with its grey leaves and yellowy mounds of flowers.

While it does best in sun, it will grow in shade, although its shape will be the poorer. Drought-tolerant and able to make the most of poor soils, it grows well in dry shade, including under leyland cypress, a no-go area for practically anything else. Looks good and grows well alongside other grey-leaved Mediterranean plants, and as a foil for pink or blue flowers. There are several good sub-species and cultivars available.

**Evergreen perennial**
**1.2 x 1m (4 x 3ft); Fully hardy**

### E. lathyrus

This is the plant that frequently seems to appear in people's gardens without them ever having planted it, usually as a result of

*Euphorbia characias*

*Euphorbia mellifera*

exposing its long-lived seed during digging operations. Its single erect stems with dark, grey-green leaves set at right angles make it invaluable as a geometric counterpoint to more typically rounded plants. Best when grown in full sun, tolerant of dry soils but short-lived, it will always self-seed, this sometimes becoming too much of a good thing. The flowers are insignificant. It is supposed to deter moles, but has never worked in my experience.

**Short-lived perennial**
**120 x 30cm (4 x 1ft); Very hardy**

### E. mellifera

Growing to almost a small tree in mild climates and a beautifully rounded mound of pale green leaves in others, it can also be grown as a rather spectacular standard. This species should be planted more often in cooler areas, its Madeiran home having unfortunately given it a reputation for tenderness. Yellow flowers in spring can fill the whole garden with the scent of honey. Needs full sun, or light shade in warm climates, and average soil moisture. It can be grown as an umbrella-shaped standard, if basal and side-shoots are removed and one stem trained to branch at the top.

**Evergreen shrub**
**3 x 3m (10 x 10ft); Slightly tender**

### E. myrsinites

Silvery leaves that whorl along trailing stems make this an unusual plant, ideal for trailing down dry banks or over walls. Yellow-green flowers are produced in spring. Like other silvery euphorbias it needs full sun, good drainage and withstands drought.

**Evergreen perennial**
**15 x 50cm (6 x 20in); Very hardy**

*Gunnera manicata*

## FASCICULARIA PITCAIRNIFOLIA

One of the hardiest members of the pineapple family, the bromeliads, this still needs a warm spot to grow in. Rosettes of dark green, somewhat prickly leaves hug the ground and eventually produce a startling red centre, out of which small blue flowers protrude. Very useful for making the garden look a lot more tropical than it really is. Needs full sun and good drainage.

**Evergreen perennial**

**40 x 60cm (16 x 24in); Slightly tender**

## FOENICULUM VULGARE
### Fennel

Fennel is another plant with two uses, as a herb and as an ornamental foliage plant. Only asparagus can rival its feathery appearance, a superb foil for flowers and for plants with bold leaves or strong forms. There is also a very attractive purple-leaved form. It thrives in any reasonably fertile soil, in full sun, and usually self-seeds, sometimes to become a nuisance. If this does happen, remove the seed heads that follow the summer-borne yellow flowers.

**Herbaceous perennial**

**180 x 75cm (6 x 2½ft); Very hardy**

## GUNNERA MANICATA

This plant will certainly make your garden look tropical, the only problem is, it might take up the entire space. This is the largest hardy perennial there is, characteristically seen by the side of lakes in grand gardens, resembling a monster rhubarb. Personally, I think it looks at its most extraordinary in spring, when the branching light green flower spikes and young leaves burst forth from enormous hairy buds like vegetable dinosaur eggs hatching. The lobed, toothed leaves can sometimes reach up to 1.8m (6ft) across (*G. tinctoria* is slightly smaller). It needs moist soil and a fairly warm climate, although it may be protected from severe frosts by folding the dead leaves over the base of the plant in autumn.

**Herbaceous perennial**

**2 x 3m (6½ x 10ft); Slightly tender**

## HEDYCHIUM
### Garland flower; ginger lily

These are a large group of tropical plants with deliciously scented flowers and foliage somewhat reminiscent of maize. There are a few that are hardy in sheltered locations and they are useful for adding an exotic touch. The large and spectacular *H. gardnerianum*, with its great orange flower clusters, is the finest if you have a warm enough garden, but the others, such as *H. spicatum* or *H. densiflorum*, are all worth growing in an exotic corner. If happy (with full sun, moist and fertile soil) they can even spread to form large clumps.

**Rhizomatous herbaceous perennials**

**100–150 x 50–100cm (3–5ft x 20in–3ft); Slightly tender to tender**

## HELLEBORUS
### Christmas rose; Lenten rose

Hellebores are plants renowned for their attractive but often subtly coloured flowers borne in late winter. But they are worth cultivating for their leaves alone. Stiff, glossy and divided, they have a robust quality that contrasts nicely with finer-leaved perennials in summer, while the evergreen forms bring interest to otherwise bare winter borders. They are not quick to grow, but once established all will thrive in sun or part shade, in fertile and not too dry soils.

Of the varieties, *H. argutifolius*, (syn. *H. corsicus*), more than earns its keep by having large greyish leaves that look at their best in winter. Pale green flowers get very few people excited but *H. argutifolius* is a particularly handsome companion to early spring bulbs. Personally, I regard it as an almost essential border plant.

*H. foetidus*, the stinking hellebore, bears green flowers that are marginally more exciting than those of *H. argutifolius*. Its foliage, though, is magnificent, certainly among the finest of any evergreen perennial. The whole plant forms a large symmetrical mound of dark green, deeply

*Helleborus argutifolius*

lobed leaves, and with grey-leaved neighbours for contrast it looks stunning, all the more so since it is at its tidy best in winter. The variety 'Wester Flisk', with very narrow leaf divisions, is one of the best of several varieties chosen for their different foliage shapes or colours. Happy in shade, including dry shade, although it will keep its shape best in the sun. Adaptable, but best on fertile and alkaline soils.

**Evergreen perennials**

**75 x 100cm (2½ x 3ft); Very to fully hardy**

## HERACLEUM MANTEGAZZIANUM

A most striking plant, a giant cow parsley that towers above all other herbaceous plants with its huge white flower heads and deeply cut fresh green leaves. Being biennial it will need propagating from seed, although it usually does this of its own accord. Unfortunately, it has attracted much bad and hysterical publicity on account of its supposed invasive tendencies and toxic properties. Both are greatly exaggerated, although people with sensitive skins should avoid touching it in hot summer weather as rashes can occasionally result. Dry seed

heads make magnificent winter decorations, either left on the plant, or cut for indoors.

**Herbaceous biennial**

**2.5 x 1m (8 x 3ft); Very hardy**

## HOSTAS
### Funkia; plantain lily

Fads and fashions come and go in gardening, much as in clothes and cars. A few years ago it was hostas; we were flooded with a vast number of varieties that all

*Hosta*

looked remarkably similar. Worse still, they were often grown together with no other plants for contrast or variation. They do have handsome foliage, but when grown *en masse* the result is as attractive as a field of cabbages. However, if combined with ferns, solomon's seal (*Polygonatum* spp.) and other plants that thrive in cool, moist, shady places, they are highly effective. There are many variegated varieties and some with bluish leaves. All have rather quiet mauvey flowers in spikes in summer. Slugs, unfortunately, adore them.

Finest, and undeniably architectural, is *H. sieboldiana*, which grows to 50 x 75cm (20 x 30in), with large, glaucous and stylishly pleated leaves. As it grows reasonably symmetrically when not hemmed in by neighbours, it looks good in a container – urns in formal settings, for instance. However, you will have to ensure that it receives enough water when grown this way.

**Herbaceous perennials**

**40 x 40cm (16 x 16in); Very hardy**

## IRIS

Not only do irises have beautiful if short-lived flowers, their neat clumps of sword-shaped leaves make an effective contrast with the foliage of the majority of perennial border plants. Most are deciduous, but not all, the small-growing Pacific coast hybrids, up to 40cm (16in), are evergreen and so are the well known bearded irises, leaves 25–75cm (10–30in) long. Whereas most species prefer the moister soils, the bearded varieties, of which there are an enormous number, are plants of poor, dry, sun-baked places. Their broad grey-green leaves add character to wherever they are planted.

**Herbaceous and rhizomatous perennials**

*Kniphofia* 'Tuckii'

*Melianthus major*

## KNIPHOFIA
### Red-hot poker; torch lily

These add a truly exotic touch to any planting, with their skyward thrusting, tight spikes of red and orange flowers. The stout rosettes of arching linear leaves have their uses too, especially in varying the pace in a border, so distinctly different are they in shape to the softer foliage of many border plants. The most distinctive of the many species and hybrids commonly available is *K. caulescens*, which grows to 1.2 x 1m (4 x 3ft) with greyish-tinged leaves and thick woody stems, quite hardy and looking like an escapee from a safari park!

**Deciduous and evergreen perennials**

**100 x 60cm (3 x 2ft); Slightly tender**

## LYSICHITON AMERICANUS
### Yellow skunk cabbage

After gunnera, this is the next largest hardy waterside plant, its vast leaves, sometimes more than 1m (3ft) long, growing out of wet ground, forming an effective weed-smothering blanket. If you have the space, it is vital for creating the primeval or tropical look. The rich yellow arum-like flowers with bold spathes (hoods) emerge from the mud before the leaves. Similar, but somewhat smaller and with white flowers, is *L. camtschatcense*.

**Herbaceous perennial**

**1 x 2m (3 x 6½ft); Very hardy**

## MACLEAYA MICROCARPA
### Plume poppy

This is one of the most elegant of perennials, as it has tall stems bearing exquisitely lobed leaves of pinkish-grey-green. The numerous but tiny flowers are oddly flesh tinted and are carried in large bunches, hence the common name. It is one of those plants that is guaranteed to bring dignity to wherever it is planted, wild garden or border, and its subtle colouring seems to go well with just about anything, both pastel or vibrant colour schemes. Spreads strongly in any soil, but prefers moist ones. *M. cordata* is very similar but spreads less widely. Sun or part shade.

**Herbaceous perennial**

**2 x 1m (6½ x 3ft); Very hardy**

## MELIANTHUS MAJOR
### Honeybush

Perhaps the finest foliage for the warm border, its large grey leaves are divided into many leaflets, elaborately toothed. Where frosts are very light, it will grow quickly into a shrub, the leaves atop a gaunt stem. The tatty charm of this arrangement may please some, but most of us will want to cut it back annually as the young growth forms the clump that gives this plant its good name. Spikes of deep-red flowers are produced in early summer. Worth any amount of effort to protect from hard frosts, but they are not otherwise fussy.

**Evergreen shrub or perennial**

**3 x 1.5m (10 x 5ft); Slightly tender**

## MUSA BASJOO
### (SYN. M. JAPONICA)
### Japanese banana

Bananas have the most quintessentially tropical foliage of all, and this one is practically hardy. The leaves are characteristically pointed and arching with deep parallel veins; they are 1m (3ft) long. Winter protection for the stem is advisable, although the plant will regenerate from the root if the top is damaged. More crucially, though, it must have protection from the wind which can shred the leaves. Needs full sun and a fertile soil.

**Evergreen perennial**

**2 x 1m (6½ x 3ft); Slightly tender**

## OPHIOPOGRON PLANISCAPUS 'NIGRESCENS'

Grassy foliage so dark as to be black: no wonder this is such a sought-after plant. It also produces mauve flowers, followed by black berries. This perennial works well with silvers, pinks and pastels or with more avant-garde foliage-based plantings and slowly spreads in sun or light shade.

**Evergreen perennial**

**20 x 30cm (8 x 12in); Very hardy**

## PAEONIA
### Peony

Peonies are grown for their voluptuous flowers, but given that so many flower for such a short time that you miss them if you blink, it is worth considering them for their foliage, which is nearly always superb. The herbaceous species and hybrids are usually bulky plants at around 60cm (2ft) high and have attractive lobed leaves, those of the yellow-flowered P. mlokosewitschii being particularly fine: grey-green with gently rounded lobes. The shrubby 'tree peonies' are woody, growing to 3m, with grandly lobed leaves, and some autumn colour.

**Herbaceous perennials, deciduous shrubs**

**Very hardy**

## PETASITES

Fluffy flowers in spring herald the later appearance of pleasingly rounded heart-shaped leaves which grow from underground rhizomes, making an attractive and effective ground-covering carpet. P. album is one of the smallest, up to 30cm (1ft) high and very shade tolerant. The others, notably P. japonicus, grow much larger, up to 75cm (2½ft) tall and spread in damp ground like wild fire. You have been warned! Good companions to gunnera and swampy plants.

**Rhizomatous herbaceous perennials**

**Very hardy**

## PHORMIUM TENAX
### New Zealand flax

This is the largest hardy plant of the 'rosette of spiky sword-shaped leaves' brigade. As such, it is invaluable in places where a look of aggressive modernity or cosmopolitan exoticism is needed. Its shape is also a welcome change from the usual rounded form of shrubs, so it is useful for changing the pace in shrub plantings. Rather odd red flowers on somewhat more impressive spikes are produced by older plants. There are a good many varieties, many smaller and often with variegated or coloured foliage, but they vary considerably in their degrees of hardiness. Shelter from cold wind, with good drainage and full sun.

**Evergreen perennial**

**1.5 x 2.5m (5 x 8ft); Slightly tender**

## PODOPHYLLUM HEXANDRUM
### Himalayan May flower

Large, lush leaves, deeply lobed, give this plant a distinctive character. Its small, pale pink flowers in spring are succeeded by large plum-like fruits in autumn. It needs

*Phormium tenax*

*Rodgersia* and ferns

shade and a cool, moist, humus-rich root run to do well, making it an excellent companion for ferns and hostas.

**Herbaceous perennial**
**50 x 30cm (20 x 12in); Very hardy**

### RODGERSIA

Noble and lush plants for waterside and cool, moist places. Their large, often bronze-tinged leaves are the main feature, although they have attractive flowers in mid-summer – large panicles of tiny cream blooms. *R. pinnata* is pink-flowered with leaves divided into leaflets off a central midrib; it is one of the smaller species. *R. aesculifolia* is one of the largest, with leaves more like that of a giant horse chestnut. *R. podophylla* is useful where a strong spreader is needed (and a lot of trouble where one isn't!). Closely related,

and needing similar conditions, is *Astilboides tabularis* which has large, round, undivided leaves, up to 90cm (3ft) across and flowers to 1.5m (4ft).

**Rhizomatous herbaceous perennials**
**100 x 60–100cm (3 x 2–3ft); Very hardy**

### SILPHIUM
### Prairie docks

These tower above other perennials, adding noble stature to prairie and wild garden plantings. However, their height and rather solitary nature makes them difficult to fit into more conventional borders. *S. terebinthaceum* has particularly large leaves, whereas *S. perfoliatum* is probably the tallest. They like full sun on fertile, moist, but well-drained soils.

**Herbaceous perennials 1.8–3m x 50cm**
**(6–10ft x 20in); Very hardy**

### UMBELLIFERS
### Cow parsley family

Cow parsleys have usually been treated with scorn by gardeners. Now, however, the new generation of planting designers is beginning to appreciate their worth. Strongly upright stems and distinctive foliage are their most desired characteristics, although the subtle flowers are also sometimes a feature. The herb lovage, *Levisticum officinale*, is a noble perennial of 2m (6½ft) in height, a worthy addition to the border. *Peucedanum verticillare*, reaching up to 2m (6½ft) in height, and *Ferula communis*, which takes several years before it grows its 3m- (10ft-) tall flower stem, are also increasingly grown. Both of these die after flowering, so the seed will have to be saved for the next generation. Sweet cicely, *Myrrhis odorata*, around 60 x 60cm (2 x 2ft), is a fine white-flowered, soft-foliaged plant for sun or light shade, while *Selinum tenuifolium*, growing to 150 x 60cm (5 x 2ft), also white-flowered, is even more highly regarded for its dark, soft leaves.

**Herbaceous perennials**
**Very to fully hardy**

### VERATRUM NIGRUM
### Black false hellebore

Few will get excited about the rather murky, dark-purple flowers of this perennial, but the leaves, neatly pleated in the manner of a well-ironed skirt, are a highly distinctive feature, along with its near upright habit. They are difficult to propagate, which makes them expensive. Best in cool, rich soils in shade. Rhizomes are poisonous.

**Rhizomatous herbaceous perennial**
**150 x 50cm (5ft x 20in); Very hardy**

*Selinum tenuifolium* (cow parsley)

# TREES AND SHRUBS

### ACACIA DEALBATA
### Mimosa

A well known tree of Mediterranean climates, with its deliciously scented flowers marking the beginning of spring, it also makes a fine tree, with grey, very finely divided foliage and a strong upright habit. Hardy in cooler localities if well positioned. Beware! It can grow frighteningly fast.

**Evergreen tree**

**10 x 6m (33 x 20ft); Slightly tender**

### A. pravissima

Hardier than A. dealbata and free-flowering with a more compact habit, it is useful against a protecting wall. Peculiar, but attractive triangular foliage. Bright yellow flowers are produced in late winter. Succeeds in any well-drained soil.

**Evergreen shrub**

**3 x 2.5m (10 x 8ft); Slightly tender**

*Aralia elata* 'Aureovariegata'

### ACER PALMATUM

Selected for centuries by Japanese court and temple gardeners the dwarf maples are plants with a special place in the garden as well as in history. Having a single trunk we can refer to them as trees rather than shrubs, despite their small size. They have a spreading habit but vary considerably in stature, from the dwarf cut-leaf forms like 'Dissectum' which, as older plants, look rather like vegetable trolls with their hair touching the ground, to what are clearly small trees, such as 'Osakazuki'. Older trees are notable for the slight zig-zag markings on the branches. These are plants grown primarily for their leaves, which vary from green through crimson to purple and come in a wide variety of shapes. All have splendid autumn colour too. They need a moist soil, preferably acid, and protection from wind and strong sun.

**Deciduous dwarf tree**

**1.5–5 x 2–5m (5–16 x 6½–16ft); Very hardy**

### AILANTHUS ALTISSIMA
### Chinese tree of heaven

Common in polluted urban environments, this carries distinctive long leaves, divided into many leaflets and up to 60cm (24in) long. It is useful for any wind-free site where a fast growing tree is wanted, or if a slightly exotic look is desired. Happy on most soils.

**Deciduous tree**

**20 x 12m (65 x 40ft); Fully hardy**

### ARALIA ELATA

A highly distinctive shrub with a single upright stem (covered in nasty spines) when young, producing a few branches later on. Eventually it will sucker, forming a small thicket. The leaves are double pinnate

which means that they divide into two sets of stems before turning into leaflets. Each leaf can be 1 x 1m (3 x 3ft). Large clusters of white flowers are succeeded by black fruits. It will do well in any reasonably moist soil. Quite fast growing when young.

**Deciduous shrub**

**3 x 3m (10 x 10ft); Fully hardy**

### ARAUCARIA
### Monkey puzzle tree

There is nothing else remotely like a monkey puzzle tree. Nothing. With its branching stems covered in dark needles, it simply has to be grown on its own, with nothing else around it to detract from its singular glory. The best specimens form a tall dome and bear branches and leaves all the way down the trunk to ground level. Very windproof, it grows best on moist but well-drained soils.

**Evergreen tree**

**25 x 10m (80 x 33ft); Fully hardy**

*Acer palmatum* 'Dissectum

## ARBUTUS
### Strawberry tree

A distinctive bendy, branching form, easily visible through the rather sparse foliage, makes these small trees highly architectural. Their red-brown bark adds further interest, along with their urn-shaped flowers and red fruits. They thrive in mild and coastal areas, and do well in light shade. Good drainage is important, but unlike most members of the ericaceae family, they do not need acid soil. *A. unedo*, *A. andrachne* and *A.* x *andrachnoides* are the most familiar, *A. menziesii* is slightly less hardy, but has wonderful bark.

**Evergreen trees**

**5 x 5m (16 x 16ft); Fully hardy**

## BUXUS SEMPERVIRENS
### Common box

An immensely popular shrub for hedging and topiary, its tight growth of dark green glossy leaves, ability to sprout from old wood and speed of growth (slow enough for topiary, fast enough to keep you interested), make it ideal for those who like creative clipping. There are several varieties, including some with variegated foliage, and a dwarf form – 'Suffruticosa' – which is useful for making the low hedges you trip over in cottage gardens! There are also several related species available from specialist nurseries, most with similar neat foliage and a tight habit. Box will grow on any well-drained soil, but the better the soil the faster the growth. It also grows surprisingly well in shade.

**Evergreen shrub**

**4 x 4m (13 x 13ft); Very hardy**

## CATALPA BIGNONIOIDES
### Indian bean tree

The catalpa is a fast growing tree with large, roughly triangular leaves of a fresh, healthy appearance. Upright in its younger years, it spreads with age, and makes a fine specimen tree for a large lawn or courtyard. Spikes of white flowers in summer are followed by distinctive long bean-like fruit. Good fertile soil is needed and protection from wind. It is capable of living to a considerable age.

**Deciduous tree**

**12 x 12m (40 x 40ft); Fully hardy**

## CHAMAEROPS HUMILIS

Essentially a shrubby multi-stemmed palm with large fan shaped leaves, and negligible, yellow flowers in summer. It works well with yuccas and other spiky plants in creating semi-desert effects. Keep out of cold winds. Not fussy about soil except that good drainage is essential.

**Evergreen palm**

**1.5 x 2m (5 x 6½ft); Slightly tender**

## CHOISYA TERNATA
### Mexican orange blossom

This is a common, easily grown and rewarding shrub. Although it is rather shapeless (and becomes worse if occasional light pruning is omitted), its small, neat, glossy leaves give it a 'lighter' and much less oppressive appearance than many evergreens, making it good for combining with herbaceous perennials in borders. There is a yellow-leaved form, 'Sundance', which to many eyes appears horribly diseased. The scented, white flowers are produced in early summer. Choisya is tolerant of shade, sun and most soils. Medium growth rate.

**Evergreen shrub**

**2 x 2m (6½ x 6½ft); Fully hardy**

## CORDYLINE AUSTRALIS

Once upon a time cordylines were seen only at coastal resorts. Now they seem to be everywhere, the quintessential 1980s yuppy plant, the rosette of arching strap-shaped grey-green leaves adding a look of dynamic energy to a planting scheme. Being such good eyecatchers means that they should be

*Arbutus* x *andrachnoides*

placed carefully as they can too easily draw all the attention to themselves. They are frequently grown in ornamental containers, but should be protected against root freezing in winter. They thrive in most soils, dry ones especially, and need full sun and protection against cold winds, although mild coastal winds and gales do little harm. 'Atropurpurea' is a brown-leaved form that is less hardy. Fast growing in mild areas.

**Evergreen shrub**

**4 x 3m (13 x 10ft); Slightly tender**

## CORNUS CONTROVERSA

A most unusual small tree which develops a 'wedding cake' framework of tiered branches, most useful for adding a formal look to woodland settings, or as a distinctive specimen plant on a large lawn. It has white

*Cotoneaster horizontalis*

flowers in spring and good autumn colour. There is also a variegated form. Succeeds in most soils, but deep fertile ones are best, in sun or light shade. Medium rate of growth.

**Deciduous tree**

**7 x 6m (23 x 20ft); Very hardy**

## COROKIA COTONEASTER
### Wire-netting bush

The common name describes it perfectly! Yellow flowers in spring and red fruit in autumn add a little decorative touch to an extraordinarily sculptural little plant. It needs acid soil. Slow growing.

**Dedicuous shrub**

**60 x 100cm (2 x 3ft); Slightly tender**

## CORYLUS AVELLANA 'CONTORTA'
### Corkscrew hazel

Lovers of natural sculpture adore this plant, while others hate it for its contortedness. Twisting branches give it character in winter, especially when adorned with catkins, but twisted leaves in summer are less attractive. It is usually grafted, so remove any suckers or shoots growing from the base, otherwise they will take over. Grows in any soil, sun or shade. Slow growing.

**Deciduous shrub**

**3 x 4m (10 x 13ft); Very hardy**

## COTONEASTER HORIZONTALIS

The fact that it is extremely common should not stop us appreciating the uniquenesss of the 'fishbone' branching habit of this robust and easy-to-please shrub. Tiny, glossy dark leaves cover the flat branches, and the pink flowers of early summer are followed by masses of small red berries in autumn. In

nature it sprawls over rocks, but can be persuaded to do the same against walls of houses, even on the shaded side. Easy to grow in any soil. Medium growth rate.

**Evergreen shrub**

**1 x 3m (3 x 10ft); Very hardy**

## CUPRESSUS SEMPERVIRENS
### Italian or Mediterranean cypress

A favourite in the Mediterranean since Roman times, this extremely ornamental, heaven-reaching conical cypress is evocative of Tuscan hillsides. Hardier than commonly thought, it deserves to be planted more widely in cooler regions. It does well on any well-drained soil, dry sites included. Keep out of cold winds and protect young plants from the worst of the winter.

**Evergreen tree**

**15 x 1.5m (50 x 5ft); Fully hardy**

## EMBOTHRIUM COCCINEUM
### Chilean fire-bush

Few hardy trees draw attention to themselves as blatantly as this with its bright orange flowers in early spring, yet this should not obscure its near erect, fanning habit, particularly useful as a contrast to the solid forms that rhododendrons habitually develop. It must have moist, but well-drained acid soil, shelter from cold winds and preferably from strong sun as well. Reasonably fast growing.

**Evergreen tree**

**8 x 4m (25 x 13ft); Slightly tender**

## ERICA ARBOREA
### Tree heather

A bushy grower with branches tending to rise upwards, this shrub is covered in white flowers in spring. It is not terribly tidy but

*Erica arborea*

makes a good contrast to the lower-growing heathers. Liable to frost and wind damage. Requires acid soil. Not a fast grower.

**Evergreen shrub**

**4 x 4m (13 x 13ft); Fully hardy**

## ERIOBOTRYA JAPONICA
**Loquat**

All too often grown unnecessarily against a sheltered wall, this bushy plant is hardier than is often thought. With leaves looking like a heavy duty version of a sweet chestnut leaf – glossy, oblong, with prominent veins – it makes a striking foliage plant. Large clusters of fragrant white flowers are carried in early autumn. Plants are most easily obtained by growing fresh seed from bought fruit, which is pear-shaped and dark yellow. Suitable for any reasonable soil. Medium growth rate.

**Evergreen shrub**

**8 x 8m (25 x 25ft), Fully hardy**

## EUCALYPTUS
**Gum tree**

Eucalyptus are rapid-growing trees with abundant, distinctive, aromatic silvery leaves, often striking pale or dappled bark and a somewhat alien appearence, although

there is no denying their attractiveness. Most have an upward-thrusting habit. Younger plants have rounded, more silvery leaves, while the adult leaves are usually longer and willow-like. In many species it is possible to maintain the juvenile foliage by cutting back to the base every few years. They are not fussy about soil, so long as it is well drained. Shelter from cold winds.

There is a bewildering number of species available, many remarkably alike, and of these there are often different clones which may vary markedly in hardiness. Seek the advice of a specialist nursery. The most commonly available species, with a range of heights and spreads, are *E. coccifera*, *E. gunnii*, *E. globulus* and *E. niphophila*.

**Evergreen trees and shrubs**

**Fully hardy to slightly tender**

## EUCRYPHIA

Eucryphias are known primarily for their wonderful, delicate white flowers that are borne in mid-summer, yet most also have a good upright habit and fine glossy dark foliage. *E.* x *nymansesnis* 'Nymansay' is thought of as the best. *E. glutinosa* is especially upright, while *E. lucida* is more rounded than most and has distinctive thick, greyish, densely packed leaves. They do best on moist, but well-drained acid soils but tolerate some alkalinity, if not too dry. Light shade is best, making them good for woodland planting. Medium growth rate.

**Evergreen trees and shrubs**

**8 x 4m (25 x 13ft); Frost hardy**

## FATSIA JAPONICA

The large, hand-shaped leaves of this relative of the ivy make it one of the most useful, very hardy plants that looks truly

*Eucalyptus perriniana*

exotic and tropical. It forms a neat, glossy, rounded shrub in sunny or partly shaded situations, with creamy white flower clusters in autumn. It looks especially good in a shaded courtyard, growing alongside ferns and hostas. Succeeds in any reasonable soil.

**Evergreen shrub**

**3 x 3m (10 x 10ft); Fully hardy**

## FICUS CARICA
**Common fig**

This fig provides not only luscious fruit (in warmer climes) but exotic-looking leaves as well. For creating a tropical effect it is arguably the most useful small tree, thriving on any well-drained soil in a spot that is protected from hard frosts and wind. Being

*Ginkgo biloba*

*Hebe*

a warmth lover it needs good light, and benefits from being grown against a wall that faces the sun. It will fruit only after long hot summers, and reliably so only in poor soils, or when the roots are restricted by being grown in a box or other container. Good yellow, autumn colour is a bonus.

**Deciduous tree**

**6 x 6m (20 x 20ft); Slightly tender**

## GENISTA AETNENSIS
### Mount Etna broom

Most brooms are somewhat untidy and short-lived shrubs. However, this one is greatly superior, forming a graceful small tree with willowy twigs sparsely clothed with tiny leaves. Its silhouette is particularly attractive. Like other brooms it flowers freely in early summer, producing yellow flowers. Native to Italy, it flourishes on dry and well-drained soils. Medium growth rate.

**Deciduous small tree or shrub**

**5 x 5m (16 x 16ft); Slightly tender**

## GINKGO BILOBA
### Maidenhair tree

Well known as the 'living fossil' upon which dinosaurs grazed, the ginkgo makes a remarkably good tree for smaller and urban gardens owing to its relatively narrow habit, broadening out only in later life. There are an increasing number of varieties that stay narrow and upright, such as 'Fastigiata' and 'Tremonia'. Not only is its outline unusual and elegant but its bright green, fan-shaped leaves – an almost unique survival of a shape common hundreds of millions of years ago – are a worthwhile feature too, turning yellow in autumn. The Japanese regard it as not only sacred, but fire-proof, planting it around temples. It does protect itself

against fire to some extent by the emergency production of watery sap. It is easy to grow in any well-drained soil. Relatively fast growing.

**Deciduous tree**

**30 x 5–10m (100 x 16–33ft); Very hardy**

## GRISELINIA LITTORALIS
### Dancing tree

There are few hardy woody plants as distinctive as this New Zealand native, with its thick glossy green leaves and sculptural branching habit. It does particularly well in mild but windy maritime climates, sometimes being used for informal hedging. Avoid cold, frosty areas and those exposed to cold winds. It is adaptable to most soils and fast growing. Tolerant of light shade.

**Evergreen small tree or shrub**

**5 x 5m (16 x 16ft); Slightly tender**

## HEBE

An extremely useful group of small or dwarf evergreen shrubs, all with attractive foliage and often flowering colourfully, usually in mid- or late summer when most shrubs have finished. Coming from New Zealand, they thrive in blustery but mild climates, making them suitable for coastal gardens. They do not do so well in continental climates, though, being intolerant of severe frosts and cold winds. As a general rule, the smaller the leaf, the hardier they are.

Hebes are pretty bewildering in the number of species and varieties available for the garden. The smaller varieties, when grown in good light, form dense rounded bushes, and these are the most architectural plants, providing squat, solid shapes in the garden. *H. sub-alpina* is particularly good, growing to around 1.2 x 2m (4 x 6½ft).

*Hydrangea quercifolia*

Denser still are the higher altitude dwarf species, sometimes called the 'whipcord hebes', after their tiny, clustered leaves, rather similar to a cypress. *H. cupressoides* 'Boughton Dome' is one of the best known, forming a tight mound of slow-growing green, to 50 x 50cm (20 x 20in), after a good few years. These dwarf hebes rarely seem to flower, incidentally, but they are an interesting alternative to dwarf conifers in combination with heathers, grasses and other heathland plants.

Hebes are not fussy about soil, so long as it is well drained, and with the exception of the dwarf species, grow at a moderate rate. Light pruning will keep them in shape.

**Evergreen small shrubs**

**Fully hardy to slightly tender**

## HYDRANGEA

There is more to hydrangeas than mop-headed bright pink and blue flowered shrubs. Not only are many of the species a lot more subtle in their beauty, but many

have very distinctive leaves, making them invaluable where bold foliage or an exotic look is required. They tolerate shade well, but need reasonably moist soils, preferably acid or only slightly alkaline.

**Deciduous and evergreen shrubs and climbers; Fully hardy**

### *H. aspera* and related species

If the epithet 'vulgar' can be applied to the bright, nodding hydrangeas then surely 'aristocratic' can be used for these. Huge, densely hairy dark green leaves on stiffly upright stems make these unforgettable plants, an effect enhanced by their mid-summer-borne flower heads, each one a wide ring of white sterile florets surrounding hundreds of mauve fertile ones. There are three very similar species; *H. aspera*, *H. villosa* and, perhaps the best, *H. sargentiana*, which are often classified as being forms of *H. aspera*. They can be slow to establish and patience is required, especially as they look like dead sticks until

they come into (rather late) leaf. But when happy, preferably in a slightly shaded spot out of the wind, they will begin to grow strongly and to sucker, eventually forming large clumps.

**Deciduous large shrubs**

**2.5 x 3m (8 x 10ft); Fully hardy**

### *H. quercifolia*

### Oak-leaved hydrangea

More conventional in form than the previous species, this makes a fine source of distinctive foliage for the smaller garden, with white flowers in summer and good orange-red autumn colour. The name is a reminder that the leaves are lobed, rather like those of the oak (*Quercus*).

**Deciduous shrub**

**2 x 2m (6½ x 6½ft) Fully hardy**

## ILEX

## Holly

There are many varieties of holly, nearly all of them decorative. The evergreen species are particularly useful as structural elements in the garden. Their fairly slow, dense growth forms neat shapes that can also be clipped very effectively.

*I. aquifolium*, 6 x 3m (20 x 10ft) is the common or English holly. Fully hardy, it is well known for its red berries, borne only on female plants. It is often seen in formal hedges, but even when unclipped, its upright growth and dark leaves make it a good framework plant. There are a number of cultivars and hybrids, many with gold or silver variegated foliage.

*I. crenata*, the box-leaved or Japanese holly is a dwarf species, only 1 x 1.5m (3 x 5ft), and more like a box than a holly, with its small, dark leaves. The dense branching and mounding habit make it a good subject for topiary and intricate clipping, but it is slow growing. There are also some variegated forms, which do best in sun or semi-shade. All prefer well-drained soil.

**Evergreen shrubs; Very hardy**

## JUNIPERUS SCOPULORUM 'SKYROCKET'

The narrowest tree there is, apart from *Cupressus sempervirens*, but better suited to severe winter climates. It makes the ideal vertical element for horizontal plantings or for any kind of exclamation mark and has attractive, scale-like foliage. Similar, but smaller, rarely exceeding 3m (10ft), is *Juniperus communis* 'Hibernica'. Full sun and any well-drained soil are needed. Moderate growth rate.

**Small evergreen conifer**
**8m x 50cm (25ft x 20in); Very hardy**

## LAURUS NOBILIS
### Bay laurel, Sweet laurel

The bay tree has one of the longest histories of any cultivated plant, having been grown by the Romans. Its oval, dark green leaves are attractive enough, but perhaps its most valuable attribute for our purposes is the ease with which it can be both clipped to shape and grown in a container. Not many shrubs make good pot plants, but bays, if well-watered and fed in summer, seem to thrive in containers, making them ideal for balconies, roof gardens and other confined spaces. They are often seen grown as standards, pyramids or balls, frequently the centre piece to a classically formal planting. If these seem like clichés, use your imagination and clip the plant into a more original shape. If grown in pots, insulation

*Mahonia japonica*

of the container is vital in winter, and all plants should be kept out of cold wind, prefering warm, moist conditions.

**Evergreen shrub**
**5 x 4m (16 x 13ft); Fully hardy**

## LIGUSTRUM LUCICUM
### Chinese privet

Privets have a bad name, a reputation for making scruffy hedges. But they should not all be maligned; this upright species produces pointed, glossy leaves and bunches of white flowers. Left to its own devices it grows quite quickly. If the side shoots are trimmed off, leaving a single stem, it comes into its own as a structural element in the garden, forming a neat, somewhat conical standard. Tolerates some shade and any reasonable soil.

**Evergreen small tree or large shrub**
**8 x 8m (25 x 25ft); Fully hardy**

## LONICERA NITIDA

This vies with privet as the 'most despised shrub', a legacy of its being the favourite small hedging plant of people who hate gardening! However, if well cared for, there is no reason why this honeysuckle should not be regarded as an alternative to box. It has tiny neat leaves and a dense twiggy habit, ideal for close clipping. It can get woody and unattractive with age, but restorative hard pruning will bring it back to shape. There is a yellow form, 'Baggesen's Gold'. It will grow on any reasonable soil and will take some shade.

**Evergreen shrub**
**1.5 x 3m (5 x 10ft); Fully hardy**

## MAGNOLIA

A versatile genus that provides us with some of our best loved flowering trees. Two species, though, are quite superlative:

*Olearia* x *macrodonta*

The first, *M. delavayi* has one of the largest leaf sizes of any hardy tree, and is an absolute must for the tropical-looking garden. Older plants bear vast creamy flowers. Warm climates will see it reach its full potential, but in other regions it will form a large shrub if it has the protection of a warm wall.

The other, *M. grandiflora,* has large, glossy, almost laurel-like leaves. Like *M. delavayi*, it has huge, white, scented flowers, and some varieties, such as 'Exmouth', will flower relatively young. Usually grown as a shrub against a warm wall, this species will take training and clipping well, and is consequently some-times seen grown as an exotic-looking climber. Fully hardy, it should be grown more frequently as a free-standing tree in cooler climates. Warm climates see it grow into a magnificent tree.

**Deciduous or evergreen trees and shrubs**

**14–15m x 8m (45–50 x 25ft); Fully hardy**

## MAHONIA

The most architectural of the shrubs commonly available from garden centres, the mahonias have long leaves divided into many holly-like spiky leaflets. Most eventually form noble, upright shrubs but they can take many years to do so. The most distinctive foliage is that of *M. lomariifolia*, with its long narrow leaves. *M.* 'Lionel Fortescue' is similar and hardier. All have yellow flower spikes in winter or early spring. The variety 'Charity' is the most easily available and has wonderfully fragrant flowers. There are also excellent Californian species such as *M. fremontii*, with grey foliage. All need good soil that does not dry out and they will tolerate some shade.

**Evergreen shrubs**

**3 x 2m (10 x 6½ft); Fully hardy**

## MYRTUS
## Myrtle

Myrtles have distinctly aromatic foliage, neat dark evergreen leaves and white flowers. In colder areas they can be grown as wall shrubs. Not fussy about soil.

*M. communis* has dark little leaves which clothe a densely branching shrub, making it a suitable subject for clipping and topiary. Slightly tender, it is quite fast growing when young.

*M. apiculata* is an attractive small tree with tiny leaves and a rather sculptural habit. It has wonderful cinnamon bark which peels off in the manner of a plane tree, revealing creamier patches below, and a rather sculptural branching habit.

**Evergreen shrubs**

**4–5 x 8m (13–16 x 10ft); Fully hardy**

## NANDINA DOMESTICA
## Heavenly or sacred bamboo

A slow growing shrub with leaves divided into small leaflets that make it look a bit like bamboo. Its eastern credentials are further enhanced by the fact that it is the traditional material for making chop sticks. The young growth is reddish in spring and the foliage turns orange in autumn. Likes any reasonable soil and does best in light shade.

**Deciduous shrub**

**1 x 1.5m (3 x 5ft); Fully hardy**

## NOTHOFAGUS ANTARCTICA
## Antarctic beech

An upright growing tree with small leaves that turn golden-yellow in autumn, notable for the remarkably zig-zag growth of its twiggy branches. Does best in a good loam.

**Deciduous tree**

**20 x 10m (65 x 33ft); Fully hardy**

## OLEA EUROPAEA
## Olive

One of the most appreciated of architectural plants, the gnarled trunks of old olive trees are admired wherever they grow. Younger trees are attractive too, with neat mounds of silver foliage. Hardier than often thought, especially if a careful choice is made of varieties. Medium growth rate.

**Evergreen tree**

**10 x 10m (33 x 33ft); Slightly tender**

## OLEARIA
## Daisy bush

These Australasian plants are spectacular in flower, smothered in white or lilac-mauve daisy-like flowers. Some have distinctive foliage too, notably the evergreen shrubs, *O. macrodonta*, which has grey-green holly-like leaves with silver undersides, and *O. nummularifolia*, with tiny, tightly packed light-green leaves. (Its botanical name means 'leaves like coins'). Suitable for any well-drained soil. Reasonably fast growing.

**Evergreen shrubs 3 x 3m (10 x 10ft);**

**Fully hardy to slightly tender**

*Phillyrea latifolia*

## OSMANTHUS DELAVAYI

Good, glossy foliage makes this a useful structural shrub, enhanced by sweetly scented flowers in spring. Similar is *O.* 'Burkwoodii', noted for its ability to do well on thin limestone soils. *O. heterophyllus* has larger, more holly-like foliage and flowers in autumn. Thrives in any well-drained soils and does best in light shade.

**Evergreen shrub**

**4 x 4m (13 x 13ft); Fully hardy**

## PAULOWNIA TOMENTOSA
## (SYN. P. IMPERIALIS)
### Foxglove tree; princess tree

Triangular leaves up to 25cm (10in) across make this tree a valuable part of the foliage repertoire and long panicles of purple flowers reinforce the tropical impression. Paulownias can be grown as single-stemmed or multi-stemmed trees, or in small gardens they can be cut back regularly to grow as shrubs. As is often the case when this is done, the size of the leaves on the new growth is larger than normal. Needs full sun and a good fertile soil. Shelter from the wind and the worst of the frosts.

**Deciduous tree**

**14 x 6m (45 x 20ft); Fully hardy**

## PHILLYREA LATIFOLIA

A relative of the olive, with dark green pointed leaves, this shrub can be clipped into shape or left to grow into its natural rounded form, which is quite sculptural anyway, reminiscent of a small holm oak (*Quercus ilex*). It tolerates most soils and is salt resistant. Medium growth rate.

**Evergreen shrub**

**3 x 3m (10 x 10ft); Fully hardy**

## PICEA OMORIKA
### Serbian spruce

The narrowest of the 'Christmas tree'-type conifers, perfect for confined spaces. Remarkably tolerant of all types of soils, including shallow limestone, it seems to grow at the same steady pace on them all. It is also pollution tolerant.

**Evergreen conifer**

**18 x 4m (55 x 13ft); Very hardy**

## PINUS
### Pine

The pines are a large, diverse, adaptable and much-loved genus of evergreen trees. For our purposes they are worth looking at in detail, because, unlike most conifers which tend to develop very symmetrically, pines as they age tend to become open in growth and asymmetric, natural plant sculptures. All are easy to grow, thriving on poor sandy soils in many cases. The following are only among the best:

### *P. parviflora*

This is the pine tree found on willow-pattern china and much of oriental art. Its layered branching on a bending trunk makes it one of the most sculptural of conifers. It is slow growing, however, and

takes many years to develop its shape. Several dwarf cultivars are available.

**Evergreen tree**

**20 x 8m (65 x 25ft); Very hardy**

### *P. pinea*
### Stone pine; umbrella pine

This is the classic Mediterranean species, although sadly much reduced in numbers in its natural habitat. Its characteristic umbrella shape is an adaptation to minimize damage to the foliage and has the advantage of creating plenty of space and light underneath. Ideal for hot climates with summer drought and poor soils, it does surprisingly well in colder areas once past the seedling phase. Its seeds are the pine kernels of Middle Eastern cuisine.

**Evergreen tree**

**20 x 10m (65 x 33ft); Fully hardy**

### *P. radiata*
### Monterey pine

Rich green needles and a good dome shape, quickly achieved, make this a valuable tree for the larger garden. It makes an excellent windbreak, especially in coastal areas.

**Evergreen tree**

**65 x 20m (215 x 65ft); Fully hardy**

### *P. sylvestris*
### Scots pine

Conical when younger but with a very open, strongly asymmetrical habit when older, the Scots pine is one of the most attractive of trees for places with very severe winters. 'Fastigiata' is an attractive upright form, rarely growing taller than 6m (20ft). Thrives on any soil other than shallow limestone.

**Evergreen tree**

**30 x 10m (100 x 33ft); Very hardy**

*Paulownia tomentosa*

*Picea omorika*

### P. wallichiana
### Bhutan pine; Himalayan pine

Long blue needles, up to 20cm (8in), draw the attention even in young plants, so this is a good choice for the impatient gardener. As it matures it develops an open shape and produces elongated, slightly curved, cones. Since individual plants can often differ considerably in how blue they are, it is advisable to select a plant carefully for its colour at a nursery. Tolerates most soils but it does need shelter from the wind.

**Evergreen tree**

**35 x 12m (115 x 40ft); Very hardy**

## PITTOSPORUM

A large group of attractive plants, of which only a few are available at garden centres. They flourish in mild or maritime areas, and on any reasonably well-drained soil. Medium growth rate.

**Evergreen small trees and shrubs**

### P. tenuifolium

Distinctive, upright habit and dense branching, together with the range of foliage colours available, make this a shrub or small tree of great potential. I have not seen it clipped, but it should be worth trying. This type has grey-green foliage with dark twigs; 'Garnettii' has white, flushed pink, variegated leaves; 'Silver Queen' is white splashed, too; 'Purpureum' is a dark brown-purple colour.

**Evergreen small tree and shrub**

**6 x 3m (20 x 10ft); Slightly tender**

### P. tobira
### Japanese pittosporum; mock orange

Suitable only for mild localities, although it does well by the coast, this species has a more sprawling, less tidy habit than *P. tenuifolium*. Its leathery leaves are elongated and dark green, the branches of creamy flowers attractively scented.

**Evergreen small tree or shrub**

**4 x 4m (13 x 13ft); Slightly tender**

## PODOCARPUS

Large, juicy needles make these very distinctive conifers, and it is a pity that they are not grown more frequently. The alpine species, at 2 x 5m (6½ x 16ft), little more than a spreading shrub, is easiest to obtain, but many species are larger, such as *P. salignus* which is 20m (65ft) tall and has long needles on pendant branches.

**Evergreen conifers**

**Fully hardy to slightly tender**

## POPULUS LASIOCARPA
### Chinese necklace poplar

A tree that looks like it has come out of a rain forest! It has some of the largest leaves of any hardy tree, up to 30cm (12in) long in sheltered conditions. It will grow on any reasonably good, well-drained soil. Slower growing than most poplars.

**Deciduous tree**

**10 x 8m (33 x 25ft); Fully hardy**

## PRUNUS
### Cherry

The cherries are well known to the point of being clichés, especially of urban planting, but they are grown this widely for very good reasons: they are fast-growing, tolerant of a wide range of soil and light conditions and of pollution. And of course the fact that they are common should not preclude the imaginative gardener from using them in new or unconventional ways.

**Deciduous or evergreen trees and shrubs**

**Fully hardy**

### *P. laurocerasus*
### Cherry laurel

This bushy shrub can grow vast and ungainly as the owners of old Victorian gardens often discover, to their cost. However, they can be cut back very severely, even to ground level, and recover quickly. They take clipping well, making good hedging plants, although if the large leaves are cut into the result looks careless and untidy. Of the varieties, 'Otto Luyken' is the best known, with smaller foliage and a maximum height of only 1.5m (5ft).

**Evergreen shrub**

**8 x 8m (25 x 25ft); Fully hardy**

### *P. lusitanica*
### Laurel, Portugal laurel

This is a much better plant for our purposes than *P. laurocerasus*, being a rich dark green, smaller and easier to prune into interesting shapes. Clipped into basic geometrical forms, it makes a good framework plant for gardens of all sizes, and for those with more confidence with the clippers, it can be made into a standard. One of the most useful aspects of this plant is its similarity to bay, and it is hardier so can be grown in colder situations where bay would rapidly turn a nasty brown.

**Evergreen small tree or shrub**

**5 x 5 m(16 x 16ft); Fully hardy**

### QUERCUS ILEX
### Holm oak

You need to wait at least 150 years before this tree reaches its prime, with its vast dome of neat, mostly oval, dark grey-green foliage carried by sculpturally bending boughs. In the meanwhile, though, it makes a good slow-growing shrub, rounded in

*Rhamnus alaternus*

*Rhododendron pseudochrysanthum*

form, and with variably shaped leaves subtly different to the majority of evergreens. The cork oak, *Q. suber*, is similar but smaller. Grows on most soils, and is especially good in exposed coastal areas, or those prone to summer drought.

**Evergreen tree**

**12 x 8m (40 x 25ft); Fully hardy**

### RHAMNUS ALATERNUS
### VARIEGATA

One of the finest variegated shrubs, it looks neither diseased nor garish like many variegated plants. Its small leaves are cream splashed with a slightly pink tinge, and clothe a compact, slightly pyramidal plant. Sometimes bears a good crop of red berries. It does need shelter, but succeeds on most soils and will grow in light shade.

**Evergreen shrub**

**2 x 2m (6½ x 6½ft); Slightly tender**

### RHODODENDRON
### (EVERGREEN SPECIES)

Very widely grown for their spring and early summer flowers, most rhododendrons look funereal and dull for the eleven months of the year that they are not in flower, especially when grown *en masse*. Not all, however, as some have wonderful foliage, and the peeling cinnamon bark of some varieties is another feature to be enjoyed.

Glaucous foliage is a fine feature of some rhododendron leaves, *R. thomsonii* being the best known. But it is the large-leaved species that are mainly of interest to us, those with large, dark, paddle-shaped leaves which help to conjure up an atmosphere of steamy exoticism. The finest and most easily found are *R. falconeri*, *R. rex*, and *R. sino-grande*, although specialist nurseries sell many others. These slowly become large plants, 3 x 3 m (10 x 10ft) or more, in the right conditions. Being from the warmer foothills of the Himalayas, they revel in mild damp climates and moist acid soils. In less suitable areas, sheltered town gardens probably offer the best hope of growing them, at least as small plants. They are utterly magnificent and worth the effort to make them happy. Hardy, but it is late frosts that can do the most damage.

Few rhododendrons have a form that can be described as neat, but *R. yakushimanum* and its hybrids are the exception,

*Taxus baccata*

forming tight hummocks of dark foliage with white or pink flowers growing to 1 x 1.5m (3 x 5ft). Many species also have attractive rust-coloured 'fur' that appears on the young growth.

**Deciduous and evergreen trees and shrubs**

## RUSCUS ACULEATUS
### Butcher's broom

A strange plant, with vertical stems that emerge from the ground, bearing spiky 'leaves' (in fact, adapted stems), slowly forming a clump. Not most people's idea of an attractive plant, but it is very useful as it likes to grow in quite deep shade, even dry shade. Suitable for any well-drained soil.

**Evergreen shrub**

**1 x 1.1m (3 x 3½ft); Fully hardy**

## SOPHORA TETRAPTERA

Yellow flowers and narrow leaves divided into many small leaflets make this a plant worth growing, but its almost unique pattern of zig-zag twigs puts it in the essential category. *S. microphylla* is slightly hardier and smaller. Needs well-drained soil and full sun in a warm spot.

**Deciduous shrub**

**3 x 3m (10 x 10ft); Slightly tender**

## TAMARIX TETRANDRA

Normally only seen at the seaside, this very attractive shrub deserves wider planting. Pinkish flowers in late summer and fine leaves, which give it its soft hazy heather-like appearance. No other plant of this stature has such a soft visual texture; very

useful for contrast in shrub plantings. Grows quite quickly in light, well-drained soils. Best in full sun, salt tolerant.

**Evergreen shrub**

**3 x 3m (10 x 10ft); Frost hardy**

## TAXUS BACCATA
### Yew

One of the most useful architectural trees because it can be clipped into practically any shape, which is just as well, as left to its own devices, it is pretty shapeless. Will even regrow from old wood. Various forms, some with golden foliage and some with an upright habit, of which the Irish yew, *T. baccata* 'Fastigiata' is the best known. Thrives on any well-drained and fertile soil, especially tolerant of thin, alkaline ones.

**Evergreen tree**

**10 x 7m (33 x 22½ft); Very hardy**

## TETRAPANAX PAPYRIFERA
### Rice-paper plant

Large-lobed leaves give this plant an exotic air, while creamy-white flower clusters add interest. Needs fertile soil, full sun and shelter, as it is susceptible to frost and wind.

**Evergreen shrub**

**3 x 3m (10 x 10ft); Tender**

## TRACHYCARPUS FORTUNEI
### Chusan palm; windmill palm

A hardy palm, essential for an exotic atmosphere or a vertical touch. Its fan-shaped leaves sit atop a trunk clothed in the rather messy brown, hairy stems of dead leaves. Easy in any well-drained soil, out of the wind. The warmer the climate, the faster the growth rate.

**Evergreen palm**

**4 x 2m (13 x 6½ft); Fully hardy**

## TROCHODENDRON ARALIODES

Attractive, rather ivy-like, leaves adorn this slow-growing tree which produces petalless, spoked green flowers in summer. Grows in most soils, but is best in full sun.

**Evergreen tree**

**10 x 7m (33 x 23ft); Fully hardy**

## VIBURNUM

A vast genus of plants, some of which are uncommon and deserve more attention. Nearly all have white flowers and red or black berries. Most have a medium growth rate.

### V. alnifolium

Leaves up to 20cm (8in) across make this a dramatic shrub for shade. In autumn the leaves turn an attractive orange-red.

Suckers form a spreading clump equally well in nearly all soil types.

**Deciduous shrub**

**3 x 4m (10 x 13ft); Very hardy**

### V. plicatum

Appealing white flowers, fresh green leaves and tiered branches. Needs space to be appreciated (and to prevent neighbouring plants from being crushed). 'Mariesii' has the best habit. Good in light shade.

**Deciduous shrub**

**5 x 6m (16 x 20ft); Fully hardy**

### V. rhytidophyllum

An example of a fine shrub given a bad reputation by being used by landscapers in unimaginative plantings. But its majestic, deeply-veined dark leaves deserve good

positioning, while the plant's bulk demands plenty of space. Large heads of creamy flowers are carried in spring. It tolerates light shade and most soils.

**Evergreen shrub**

**5 x 5m (16 x 16ft); Very hardy**

### V. tinus
### Laurustinus

A very well known shrub that never seems to lose its appeal, despite being widely planted. Quite apart from its smart glossy leaves and tidy habit, it produces large quantities of white flowers at a time when we most appreciate them – mid- to late winter. 'French White' is especially vigorous, 'Gwenllian' slightly smaller, while 'Lucidum' is a vigorous form with big glossy foliage. Prefers well-drained soil in sun.

**Evergreen shrub**

**4 x 3m (13 x 10ft); Fully hardy**

## YUCCA

Yuccas are the hardiest and most easily available spiky rosette plants, so essential for creating exotic-looking plantings and for adding spice and dynamic energy to any design. They are highly effective as eyecatchers, standing out dramatically from their leafier surroundings. Most bear creamy white flowers in hot summers. *Y. filamentosa*, *Y. flaccida* and *Y. gloriosa* are the most easily found and the hardiest, but specialist nurseries sell others, some very hardy but others needing warm climates. All need full sun and very good drainage. The tips are sharp and can cause injury, so position them carefully.

**Evergreen shrubs**

**2 x3m (6½ x 10ft); Fully hardy**

*Viburnum plicatum* 'Rowallane'

*Yucca filamentosa*

# APPENDIX

Since this is not a 'how to garden' book, there is no point in repeating information easily found elsewhere. However, there are some considerations that do seem to have particular relevance to architectural and foliage plants. Since there is a tendency for people to get somewhat carried away with plant buying, I have included a section on plant selection and also one on hardiness, as there are so many tempting species that are on the tender side. Finally, there is some advice on selecting and pruning hedges, making standards and creating topiary.

## CHOOSING PLANTS FOR YOUR ENVIRONMENT

Selecting architectural plants may seem to be primarily an exercise of aesthetic judgement, but it is best not to get too carried away. The hard reality is that, like anything to do with gardening, there are practical considerations of the 'will it grow' variety. Although we can alter growing conditions to some degree to suit particular plants, these are often only short term solutions. Working with nature, rather than against it, is always cheaper, involves less work and is less environmentally damaging. Deciding if it is worthwhile trying to alter your garden environment needs careful consideration, particularly of the factors that limit plant growth.

As an example, suppose you have a passion for growing the large-leaved Himalayan rhododendrons like *R. sino-grande*. If you live in a mild climate with plenty of year-round rain, you have satisfied two criteria for these plants' well being. However, let us suppose you live on a windy

clifftop, which will tear their big leaves to shreds. Since few people like sharing their lives with raging gales anyway, it is sensible to think about a windbreak. A screen can be erected in the short term and fast-growing, wind-resistant trees planted for the long term. Now, you might well be able to grow the long-desired rhododendrons. But if your soil is thin and alkaline (calcareous or limy), you should forget it. Even if you use vast amounts of acidity-creating chemicals and tonnes of peat (destroying natural habitat by so doing), you will make no long term changes, as alkaline groundwater will always be introducing lime. If you still want to grow these rhododendrons you will have to be happy with them in containers.

As water resources become increasingly scarce and awareness grows about environmentally damaging activities (such as peat digging and the over-use of fertilizers), we need to understand the habitat our gardens offer and to choose plants appropriately.

The good news is that the numbers of plants available commercially is steadily increasing. Plants that were rare a few years ago are now found far more frequently, and in some cases it is now legal to bring plants from abroad. And, equally, it is possible to control and alter your garden environment in useful ways while protecting your plants against harsh weather.

## THE WIND AND THE COLD

These are two factors which it is possible to do something about. We have a particular interest in doing so, since the more sheltered the garden, the wider the range of interesting architectural plants that we can grow, large-leaved exotic-looking subjects in

particular. Wind can damage plants in three ways: the first is physical damage, when plants are blown over and thus dislodged or broken; secondly, wind chill, that is, the effective reduction in temperature caused when air passes over living tissue (plant or human); and thirdly, salt damage, which can also be caused inland by seaborne winds.

Physical and salt damage are primarily problems in westerly facing maritime climates, and there are plenty of plants (many from New Zealand) that can cope with these factors but are badly affected by severe frosts or by wind chill. Wind chill mainly occurs in regions with a continental climate or on easterly coasts, and is anathema to many plants, especially evergreens.

Plants can be protected against any kind of wind by effective wind screens such as hedges, windbreaks or artificial barriers. Walls and solid barriers create eddies and are thus less effective than barriers that allow some air to pass through.

Aside from the wind, frost is another critical factor. The science of plant hardiness and frost is very complicated. In understanding how frost affects plants we need to bear in mind the following points:

Cold air sinks, flowing like a liquid down sloping ground. Therefore, the worst place for frosts are valley bottoms (so called frost hollows), then level ground; the best places are slopes, where cold air can drain away.

However, since land loses heat much more quickly than water, a large body of water, such as a lake, can often moderate the chill, at least until it freezes over. Being by the sea considerably reduces the danger of frost, despite the fact that cold air tends to flow towards the coast at night. This is why small islands are often the warmest places.

Frost is produced primarily by the earth and plants radiating heat upwards during clear winter nights. For this reason, any sort of cover, even something as insubstantial as the branches of a deciduous tree, can reduce heat loss. This is an important point to bear in mind when we consider how to protect plants against frost.

Water-logged conditions aggravate frost damage to plants. Light sandy soils and stony ones that drain freely offer better protection to tender plants than soils that retain water. This is part of the reason why many plants are more badly affected by light frosts in wet climates than they are by heavier frosts in dry ones.

The sun is strongly angled in winter, warming some places much more than others during the day. During this time thawing out is more rapid and there is also a greater build up of heat in the ground which keeps plants warm at night. A slope facing the sun is especially favourable.

Following on from all of these points, it is clear that the ideal place for a plant to grow is against a large tank of water facing the sun some way up a slope! Since this is not very practicable, a thick wall to act as a heat store will do instead. No wonder, then, that slopes and walls that face the sun are such favoured choices for gardeners and fruit growers. The other advantage of such a site is that it is hotter in summer when the plants are actively growing, an obvious stimulant for plants from warmer climates but also advantageous for producing the sun-ripened growth that will be more resistant to cold weather.

## PROTECTING PLANTS FROM WINTER COLD

Common sense dictates that we should select totally hardy plants for major structural elements like trees or hedges, leaving the tender experiments to the details, so that if a bad winter strikes we do not lose too much of the garden.

Tender plants may be protected from winter frost in a number of ways. How practical they are will usually depend on the size and number of plants involved in a particular planting scheme.

### Insulating with straw, bark chippings, bracken or similar material

*Useful for*: Plants that die down in winter, such as completely herbaceous perennials like cannas and hedychiums. These can be totally insulated by a thick layer of material, held in place by wires, bricks, string and so on. This form of insulation can also be used to protect the bases of shrubbier plants so that if the top is lost the roots are saved, allowing for regeneration. Another variant is to use straw matting wrapped around plants such as cordylines and palms, although this is advisable only in climates where cold is continuous and dry, as mild and wet spells will encourage fungal infection or even premature growth.

*Disadvantages*: Encourages slugs. Light material blows around the garden, or worse, your neighbours' gardens!

*Hedges provide natural protection for weaker plants while enhancing the garden's structure*

### Insulating with bubble plastic

*Useful for*: Bubble plastic can be combined with loose material, holding it in place. A very good insulator, it is easy to keep in place if it is weighed down with wire or stones.

*Disadvantages*: Can make for very humid, fungus-inducing conditions, especially in mild spells. Looks awful!

### Covering with 'mini-greenhouses' such as glass cloches

*Useful for*: Plants with parts above ground that need protecting. Bubble plastic stapled to wooden frameworks, such as vegetable boxes, is a good cheap alternative to the traditional glass cloche. Plants growing against walls can be protected, if they are not too large, by leaning a plastic-covered framework against the wall.

*Disadvantages*: Gales will blow plastic constructions all over the garden unless they are well made and well secured.

### Digging up and bringing inside

*Useful for*: Anything small enough to fit into a greenhouse or cold frame or which can be cut back. The Victorians were very keen on 'bedding out' exotic foliage plants such as agaves, bananas and palms for the summer, and many plants were kept going for many years by overwintering them under cover.

*Disadvantages*: Unsuitable for anything that dislikes root disturbance. Plants also tend to get larger from year to year which can pose problems moving and positioning them.

### Propagation

*Useful for*: Tender species, as an insurance policy. Cuttings can be taken in the summer and kept inside over the winter. If the parent plant survives the winter, give surplus plants to friends – then, if the original plant dies, you can always claim some cuttings back!

*Disadvantages*: Of limited use for architectural plants which tend not to be for short term effect, unlike patio plants (marguerites, osterspermums and the like) which are ideally suited to propagation.

## PLANTS IN CONTAINERS

It seems to have been fashionable to grow certain formal plants like box and standard bay trees in pots for a very long time. Recent years have seen cordylines and agaves join them, container and plant forming an effective focal point. Growing plants in containers has the advantage that it stops the specimen getting too large; the pot can also be moved around as often as convenience and changing ideas on design dictate, and of course it can be brought indoors for the winter.

Plants in containers are not in touch with the earth and so will need feeding during the growing season. Weekly feeding is incredibly tiresome, but it is now possible to get long-lasting nutrient pellets that can be dug in around the base of the plant in spring and will last until autumn. They, and any feed, should be well balanced, including nitrogen, phosphorus and potash (potassium) in roughly equal measure.

The main risk to plants in containers is their vulnerability to the weather. Their roots can heat up and dry out in summer much more quickly than in the ground and

*Topiary spheres form an immaculate boundary – a contrast to the angles of the path.*

likewise freeze more severely in winter. Care should be taken that any plants that sit baking in the sun all day can take it; anything listed in a reference book as being moisture- or shade-loving (such as a hosta) may not survive. Country of origin is a useful guide as well, as this will give you a good idea about the conditions the plant prefers or will tolerate. Winter chilling may be avoided by wrapping the pot in several layers of bubble plastic or another insulator.

## PRUNING AND TRAINING

While some shrubs are inherently architectural, others have to be made so. Pruning and clipping are the chief means to this end. Most shrubs, which are by nature untidy growers, can be made to grow in neater and more sculptural shapes, and the denser their habit of growth the more successful this will be and the more detailed the design can be. Annual clipping will build up a dense network of branches.

The exceptions tend to be those species with a strongly upright habit (such as philadelphus) or those that produce few branches (for example, roses). There is also little point in trying to shape shrubs with uninteresting foliage, especially since it will reduce flowering. There are few sights as irritating as the garden where everything has been clipped into a neat and tidy shape, regardless of what it is! While it is possible to clip species with large leaves such as laurels, the result is often a mess of cut and torn leaves; better to prune them and worry less about geometry.

Pruning and clipping can be done at any time of year, although the spring, when sap is rising rapidly, should be avoided, as should very hot weather and frosty weather.

As a very general rule, flowering shrubs should be pruned just after the blooms have finished, but if you want flowers the following season it is important to know whether a plant flowers on new growth or on the previous year's growth, so do consult a guide to pruning.

Shrubs and trees that are suitable for cutting into basic shapes are good for formal hedges too, dense growth making not only a functionally thick barrier but an attractive matt background to the garden. While different species do have different optimal planting distances, as an approximate guide, the narrower the hedge you want the closer together the plants should be (this will automatically restrict the growth of each plant widthways).

Most of us want our hedges to grow as quickly as possible, so thorough and deep soil preparation, including the addition of plenty of compost and feed, followed perhaps by annual manuring or feeding, is important. As the hedge grows it can be encouraged to form bushy growth by light pruning, with harder clipping once it reaches the desired dimensions. When it has reached these limits it is advisable to cut once a year to maintain dense twiggy growth. If you have planted a leyland cypress, it must be cut back ruthlessly, perhaps even twice a year.

Old hedges that have become disorderly and gappy, including laurel, yew and box, can generally be regenerated by cutting back into the wood, followed by generous feeding to encourage new growth. Such a drastic operation is perhaps best done in two stages, with one side of the hedge cut back into the wood one year and the other the next, or even the year after.

Topiary is one stage on from cutting woody plants into basic shapes, and, as it requires more fine detail, it is vital that the species chosen have dense, branching growth. The corollary of this growth pattern is that they are often relatively slow growing, which means that patience is required. Yew and common box, *Buxus sempervirens,* are the classic topiary materials in cool temperate climates and both can be persuaded to grow at a reasonable pace if given sufficient moisture and nutrients. The Japanese also use a box, *Buxus microphylla,* and a holly, *Ilex crenata,* but these are much slower growing. Other possibles are *Lonicera nitida* and privet, *Ligustrum ovalifolium,* which are good despite a reputation for looking scruffy: more to do with the places and manner in which they are usually grown (as poor, ragged hedges in unimaginative, suburban gardens), than the intrinsic character of the species.

Topiary is a complex subject, and a serious venture into green sculpture needs careful study. Briefly, though, there are two approaches to shaping plants. One is to study a plant rather in the manner of a Chinese jade carver, to see what the growth of the plant suggests. A strong diagonal branch, for example, might hint at a chicken's tail and a bunch of twigs at the top at its head. Clipping can then follow on from these natural characteristics and the form will slowly emerge, perhaps over a number of years for larger pieces. The other way is to use wire shapes – from the simple to the intricate – placed around the plant to guide the shears, anything projecting being cut off. At its simplest, a circular piece of wire is most useful for guiding the creation and maintenance of a perfect sphere.

# INDEX

# PHOTO ACKNOWLEDGEMENTS

**Listed by photographer's name followed by garden designer or location**

p1 Steve Wooster;
p2 Jerry Harpur/Eck and Winterowd;
p3 Jerry Harpur

**Introduction**
p7 Steve Wooster;
p8 Jerry Harpur/Barnsley House;
p10 Piet Oudolf;
p11 Steve Wooster; p12 Steve Wooster (pic and duotone);
p13 Steve Wooster; p14 Jerry Harpur/Eck and Winterowd;
p15 (duotone) Jerry Harpur/ Ryoan-Ji Temple; p17 Steve Wooster/ Hadspel House;
p18–19 Jerry Harpur/Bruce Kelly;

**Chapters 1–4**
p21 Jerry Harpur/ Nick and Pam Coote; p22 Jerry Harpur/ Manor House, Bermuda;

p23 Andrew Lawson/The Garden House; p24–25 Jerry Harpur/ Cranborne Manor; p26–27 Jerry Harpur/Jill Billington; p28 Jerry Harpur; p29 Jerry Harpur; p30 Andrew Lawson; p31 Andrew Lawson; p32 (duotone) Andrew Lawson, (left) Jerry Harpur/Ryl Nowell; p33 Jerry Harpur/The Dingle, Welshpool; p34 Jerry Harpur/ Simon Hopkinson; p35 Steve Wooster; p36 Noël Kingsbury; p37 Andrew Lawson/ Antony Noel; p38 (top) Steve Wooster/Beth Chatto Garden, (bottom) Steve Wooster, (main) Andrew Lawson; p39 (top) Andrew Lawson, (bottom) Noël Kingsbury; p40 (left) Jerry Harpur/ Mark Rumary, (duotone) Jerry Harpur/Wollerton Old Hall; p41 Jerry Harpur/Wollerton Old Hall; p43 Jerry Harpur/ Hatfield House; p45 Steve

Wooster; p46 Andrew Lawson; p49 Jerry Harpur/ Manor House, Bledlow; p50 Jerry Harpur/Mark Rumary; p52 Andrew Lawson; p53 (duotone) Jerry Harpur/ Rousham House; p54–55 Piet Oudolf; p56 Andrew Lawson/Bickleigh Castle, Devon; p58–59 National Trust Photographic Library/ Andrew Lawson/Hidcote, the Winter Garden; p60–61 Clive Nichols/ Crathes Castle Garden, Scotland; p62 Andrew Lawson; p64–65 Jerry Harpur/Hatfield House; p66 Steve Wooster/Beth Chatto; p67 Piet Oudolf; p68–69 Jerry Harpur/Manor House, Bledlow; p71 Steve Wooster; p72 Steve Wooster; p73 (duotone) Steve Wooster; p74–75 Jerry Harpur/Butch Joubert; p76 Andrew Lawson, (duotone) Piet Oudolf; p77 Andrew Lawson;

p78 (far left) Jerry Harpur/ Beth Chatto, (bottom right) Andrew Lawson, (main top) Andrew Lawson; p79 (left) Steve Wooster, (right) Andrew Lawson; p80–81 (duotone) Steve Wooster; p81 Jerry Harpur; p82–83 Jerry Harpur/Gunilla Pickard; p84–85 National Trust Photographic Library/Stephen Robson/Ham House; p87 Jerry Harpur/ Saling Lodge, Essex; p88 Jerry Harpur/Great Dixter; p89 Jerry Harpur/Jason Payne; p90 Jerry Harpur/Isobelle Greene; p93 Jerry Harpur/Japanese Stroll Garden; p94–95 Jerry Harpur/Ryoan Ji-Temple; p96 (duotone) Piet Oudolf/ Van Steeg; p97 Andrew Lawson; p98 (top left) Steve Wooster, (top middle) Jerry Harpur, (right) Andrew Lawson, (bottom) Steve Wooster; p99 Jerry Harpur/Lower

Hall, Worfield; p101 Jerry Harpur/Dolwen; p102 Jerry Harpur/Joe Eck and Wayne Winterowd; p103 Jerry Harpur.

**Plant Directory**
All pictures for Plant Directory courtesy of Andrew Lawson except the following
p110 (right) Garden Picture Library/Caroline Weymouth, Wimbledon;
p112 (top right) Jerry Harpur;
p121 Jerry Harpur/ Sheila Chapman;
p123 Harry Smith;
p135 Garden Picture Library/Linda Burgess.

**Appendix**
p139 Jerry Harpur/ Manor House, Bledlow;
p140 Jerry Harpur/ Ryoan-Ji Temple.